Also By Christine Kloser

BEYOND MINDSET
Everyday Inspiration to Help You Remember
What Your Heart Already Knows

CONSCIOUS ENTREPRENEURS
A Radical New Approach to Purpose, Passion and Profit

THE FREEDOM FORMULA
How to Put Soul in Your Business
and Money in Your Bank

ALIGN, EXPAND AND SUCCEED
Shifting the Paradigm of Entrepreneurial Success

INSPIRATION TO REALIZATION
Real Women Reveal Proven Strategies for Personal,
Business, Financial and Spiritual Fulfillment

PEBBLES

in the

POND

Transforming the World

One Person at a Time

TRANSFORMATION BOOKS

York, PA

Published by:
Transformation Books
211 Pauline Drive #513
York, PA 17402
www.TransformationBooks.com
ISBN: 978-0-9851407-1-7

Library of Congress Control No: 2012935562

Cover design by Sarah Barrie
Design layout and typesetting by Glen M. Edelstein
Editor: Marlene Oulton

Printed in the United States of America

A portion of the proceeds from the sale of this book will be donated to the charities the publisher supports.

Help Me Be...

Strong enough to be vulnerable.

Wise enough to realize how little I know.

Loving enough to embrace my "enemy."

Tender enough to be powerful.

Smart enough to realize I can't do it alone.

Brilliant enough to shine the light of others.

Doubtful enough to know the power of faith.

Courageous enough to share my truth.

~CHRISTINE KLOSER

Table of Contents

Introduction

"A small body of determined spirits fired by an unquenchable faith in their mission can alter the course of history."

~ Gandhi

THANK YOU FOR FOLLOWING THE WHISPER in your heart to pick up this book and crack open the cover. My guess is — like the contributors to this book — you've been on a powerful, transformational journey that sometimes joyously surprises you, and other times throws you an unexpected curve ball that knocks you to your knees.

Perhaps as you read this you're in the middle of the most challenging time of your life. Or maybe you've just come through a difficult situation with a renewed sense of faith and hope. Perhaps you have a niggling sense that a growth opportunity is lurking around the corner waiting for you, but you just don't know what it is yet.

No matter where you stand right now on your path, I trust that since you're here — taking time to read this book — you believe in the concept of a "Pebble in the Pond," and share in my vision of a world that is transformed one person at a time. Thank you for that.

While world transformation may seem like a far-fetched dream, the truth I've come to know is that as we transform as individuals, we DO make a difference in the lives of those around us. And, if you've ever thrown a stone in a still pond, you know that one single splash sends ripples outward in every direction, creating more and more ripples. It's the same thing when that "splash" is the impact of your life and how you live it each and every day. The impact expands.

It doesn't matter if you're a leading-edge entrepreneur, school-teacher, mom, rocket scientist, doctor, writer, healer, manager, sales-person, nurse, volunteer, retiree, or anything else. Your life – and how you live it – can be a force for good in our world. Every person has the power to make a difference, including you, and that's exactly what this book is about.

At this time in history, we are on the precipice of experiencing the new world many people have been dreaming about – a world filled with love, cooperation, contribution, service, community, and abundance for all. And there's a growing number of people who are doing all they can to heal themselves, become a part of the solution (simply by being who they truly and authentically are), and bring more light and love into the world.

In the pages of this book, you will meet visionary leaders and world-changers. You may recognize some of the contributors as bestselling authors and leading entrepreneurs. Others aren't as well known, yet their stories are testaments to the power of one person's transformational journey to send ripples of good into the world.

I personally feel so blessed to receive the gift of working very closely with most of the contributors to this book. We held each other close over the course of eight months to birth this book in service to you. As you discover each contributor's story, you'll see why I con-sider it a blessing to call them my clients, soul travelers, and friends. This book is only possible because of the love and light they bring to the world.

Some chapters will make you cry, while others will make you laugh. Some will touch your heart deeply, while others will inspire you to think differently. Some chapters will be difficult to read as you hear of the challenges some of the authors have faced that nobody should ever have to live through. And others will offer you a heartfelt reassurance that if they can do it (whatever the "it" is), you can, too.

So as you proceed through this book, don't feel the need to read the chapters in order. Chances are as you peruse the table of contents or randomly flip open the pages, you will receive exactly the message that is meant for you in that moment. Let your experience in reading this book be exactly right for you.

And to help you make the most of your journey as a Pebble in the Pond, here are a few resources that will deepen your experience of this book:

» *Facebook* - Please introduce yourself to me and the contributors by joining our online community at www.facebook.com/pebblesinthepond. We can't wait to see you there and hear about your experience reading this book.

» *YouTube* - If you ever need a boost of inspiration beyond what lies in the pages of this book, be sure to subscribe to the Pebbles in the Pond Channel at www.YouTube.com/pebblesinthepondbook where we're constantly adding new videos to support and serve you in your (and our world's) great transformation.

» *Free Reader Resources* -Learn more about each of the contributing authors and check out some of the valuable (and free) resources they've made available for you to further support you on your transformational journey. You can learn more about each of them by reading their bios at the end of each chapter.

» *Reading Group* - One of the most powerful ways to read and experience this book is in a community with like-minded friends where you can discuss the stories together. So choose a few friends (or start a reading group on Facebook), and discuss the chapters together. You'll see miracles occur through the conversations that unfold.

Above all else, let the stories in this book bathe you in love, compassion, understanding, and inspiration to transform your challenges and struggles (large or small) into beautiful blessings for yourself and others.

You never know what miracle may happen as a result of reading one of these stories. In fact, this book in and of itself is evidence of the miraculous grace that appeared during the most challenging time of my life. You'll learn more about it in the first chapter of this book, titled "The Best 'Worst' Time of My Life."

On behalf of myself and all of the contributing authors, we send you our deepest blessings that this book delivers the inspiration and transformation your soul is seeking. May you be guided by grace.

Love and blessings,

Christine Kloser,
Spiritual Guide ~ Award Winning Author
Transformational Book Coach ~ Publisher
Creator, www.TransformationalAuthor.com

The Best "Worst" Time of My Life

Christine Kloser

GOD SURE HAS A FUNNY WAY OF WORKING in our lives. Being a coach for years, and the author of *The Freedom Formula: How To Put Soul in Your Business and Money in Your Bank*, one of my core teachings was that the Universe is always conspiring for your highest good. It wasn't until I was put to the test in 2010 and 2011 that I discovered that I barely knew what that really meant.

Let me share some background as I guide you through the greatest faith walk of my life. This is a story I hope will help you see that even the darkest times of your life are filled with an abundance of light and the unfolding of a glorious mystery that can deliver blessing and miracles that far exceed your greatest dreams.

After being an entrepreneur since 1991, I finally hit what most would consider the jackpot in January of 2009: a successful coaching business, lots of new clients eager to work with me, a bestselling book, and generating nearly a half million in revenues in a single weekend during a seminar I hosted in Los Angeles. I also co-owned a company that trained non-fiction authors to write, publish, and market their books, and had manifested the perfect business partner to help me with that business, which I'd started in 2004. Life was good as I sailed off to the Caribbean to celebrate my success with my husband and daughter. A picture perfect life, indeed. Or was it?

Let's see. That half million dollars of seminar revenue cost nearly $150,000 to produce. I ended up with $100,000 in uncollectible credit card charges as the credit crunch hit everyone hard, including many of my clients. I had paid far more than my budget could reasonably cover to hire high-level coaches to help me reach that goal. And my credit card bills were scary proof of how much I had overleveraged myself in hopes of being a big success.

To everyone else, it looked like I had succeeded. But what kind of success was it when I put everything on the line to create the business I thought I should create – doing what so many other coaches helped people do – namely, make more money? Once I got honest with myself, I saw the truth that helping other people make money was never a passion that truly inspired me.

Transforming people's lives was my driving force. Returning people to the magnificent truth of who they really are was my gift. Helping people reclaim and shine their brightest lights in the world was my unique blessing. But I had stepped away from this truth. And I didn't trust that it was enough to make a great living. ("Not enough" was a theme I was all too familiar with, having been a high-achieving performer my whole life as a cover for the deep-seated belief that I was never going to be "enough.")

Hindsight Is Always 20/20

Little did I know that stepping away from my deepest passion would be the very thing that led me down the path of financial ruin – an experience that terrified me. Wasn't money the only measure of success that really mattered? It was in the world I grew up in, and financial ruin was the worst possible thing that could ever happen to a person in my mind. Who was I if I wasn't a financial success? What a powerful question!

After months of going through the mental, spiritual, financial, and personal anguish of realizing I had to file for bankruptcy, I felt my life was nearly over. How could I ever succeed again? Who would want to listen to what I had to say? I was a supreme failure. Maybe I should give up my dreams. How much worse could it get?

Well, maybe not that much worse, because I still had my business partner and my small publishing company. That was the only shred of hope I had to get me through those very dark days. I knew I could double our revenues in 2011 and get myself and my family back on our feet. Thank you, God, for saving this one asset in all that we were going through!

Wait! What is this? A FedEx package the day before I'm going to sign my bankruptcy papers? It's from my business partner's attorney saying she wants to buy me out of the company. What? That was the only bit of stability that remained in my life. Even my marriage was on rocky terrain after all we'd gone through. If I didn't have that company, I had nothing.

This unexpected news (after months of planning with our attorney to protect the publishing company through the bankruptcy) impacted me more deeply than finding out that my second pregnancy had ended in a miscarriage. It knocked me to my knees with a force that threw me down into darkness, pain, betrayal, and fear I'd never experienced before.

There were many days I thought I'd be better off giving up and crawling under a rock for the rest of my life. There were days I sobbed without end. There were days I couldn't recognize myself through the rage that coursed through my veins. There were times I felt like a monster for having the thoughts I had. There were days I hated God. And there were days I prayed for God to remove the hate and fear from my heart. These were the worst days of my life. And they were the best days of my life.

A Walk of Faith

In the depth of that darkness, when it appeared I had nothing left, I discovered that I had everything if I had my faith and trusted that the Universe really WAS conspiring for my highest good all the time! (Remember, I'd taught this stuff for years, but was only now being asked to really LIVE it.)

Through the mess, the fear, and the pain, a healing and transformation happened that feels like a miracle to me. On January 20th, 2011, I surrendered my personal will and leaped into trusting God fully when I stopped fighting to try to keep my publishing company and sold my shares to my partner for a price that didn't even cover my attorney's bill. It was the scariest and most liberating thing I'd ever done! I'd never exercised faith like this before. I felt like I was on a wild adventure, with God at the helm!

Letting go of that company meant I had no source of income — no business at all. I had to rely completely on the Divine to help me navigate the new and unknown terrain of my life and whatever new business was trying to emerge through me. I found an inner strength, confidence, and wisdom I'd never known before, and I promised God that I would use this experience in the highest service to others.

And that's exactly what I did. Within weeks of signing the final papers with my former business partner (and also our final bankruptcy papers), it was clear exactly what I was being prepared to do! I had been guided every step of the way, and received more miracles and blessings than I can count, which led me to launch a new business that was totally aligned to my unique gifts and blessings.

My new co-creation (this time around, my business partner is God) is in service to visionary leaders who want to share their transformational stories through the power of the written word – their books! This business is my bliss. By the grace of God, I get to channel all of my passion for helping others heal, transform, and shine, ultimately for the purpose of helping all of humanity heal, transform, and shine. And I now combine these blessings with my practical know-how of what it takes to write, publish, and market a book. Calling this new evolution of my work a "match made in heaven" is an understatement. For me, this felt like nothing short of a miracle that had been in the making for years, if not lifetimes.

The book you're now holding in your hands is evidence of that miracle, as all of the contributing authors will attest to. This is one of many tools for transformation that was birthed through the best "worst" time of my life. Don't underestimate the power of this manifestation in your hands right now. You were asking for a prayer… this just might be it!

This book is proof of the incredible gifts that await you when you surrender to a higher purpose and do what you are truly here to do, with God by your side. I never dreamed my business could be this good, this joyous, this blissful, this rewarding, this impactful, and this abundant!

Let this book (and all of the powerful stories in it) be a sign of grace in your life. Open yourself up to seeing the miracles on the pages. Believe that no matter what challenge you are facing right now, you can transform through it into a whole new experience of yourself.

This is how you create ripples of good as you drop your own pebble in the pond. This is what it's all about.

Namaste.

Christine Kloser is a spiritual guide, award-winning author, and Transformational Book Coach whose spot-on guidance transforms the lives of visionary entrepreneurs and authors around the world. She's fast become the leader of the Transformational Author Movement, teaching thousands of aspiring authors how to write, publish, and market books that make a difference. Check out excerpts from Christine's book *Beyond Mindset* at www.BeyondMindset.com. And if you want to get started writing your own transformational book, visit www. EasyBookWritingHelp.com

~2~

You Can't Make an Omelet without Breaking an Egg

Rabbi Ann White, JD

EACH NIGHT I WALK INTO THE TRAUMA UNIT of our busy hospital and am amidst blood and other bodily fluids; broken bodies and shattered dreams; prayers for the dying, for the living, and for miracles. And as I sit with those who are devastated by these sudden losses, I sometimes recall my own earlier brokenness as I merge my spirit with theirs to soothe and provide solace.

We are all broken in one way or another. The planet is broken. The Universe explodes frequently in chaos only to form new creations. Chaos and creation are part of our universal rhythm. You can't make an omelet without breaking an egg.

Breaking an Egg

Ten years after my mother died of hypochondria, my father told me that he was not really my father. From that point on, the life that I thought was mine disintegrated like burning paper, with memories floating away in the wind.

I never liked my father, and I guess since he always knew "the secret," he never liked me very much either. So in some sense, it was a relief to know that I was not biologically connected to this man who had abused me until I was old enough to keep out of the house whenever possible, at about age fourteen.

My mother knew about the abuse, and I always wondered why she never protected me or tried to stop it. I guess because of "the secret," she felt it was his prerogative to take out his anger on me. It was either me or her, and she chose me.

I have come to believe that most families are dysfunctional, so I don't claim any award for the dysfunction of my own. My mom did some "mom" things: she made fudge, played Hearts with me, we'd cut paper dolls out of newspaper together, but she was never able to guide or teach me the positive ways of the world. Obviously, neither could my dad.

When I was in my early twenties and my life was crashing down all around me, I came to a crossroad – either life or death. I told myself that if I chose life, it had to be a rich, full, and vibrant one, not just an existence. I knew right there and then that I had to nurture and teach myself since no one else would. I had to create my life as if I were making a work of art.

An Omelet in the Making

And what did I discover as I began to create this luscious life? That it all boils down to the concept of "One." This is also how I understand the drama and trauma of my job as a trauma chaplain. We are all parts of the "Oneness." Let me explain, since there are many "Ones" that merge into the "Great One."

I came to believe in a power greater than myself; a power greater than all of us; greater than everything, and a power that embodies everything. Call this power God, Spirit, Energy, Source, or even Bob, its name does not make any difference. Just know that it is, and it has a rhythm and flow of order and goodness.

All of life flows from this energetic field or Source. When we get disconnected from this Source, we feel alienated and alone. Evil and meanness are offshoots which are a product of disconnection from this Source.

We come to Earth in earth bodies from this Source. What makes us unique and gives us personality is our spirit, our energy, and it is derived from this Source. We come to earth to learn lessons or to teach them, for reasons or seasons. And when our work is complete, our lessons learned or taught, our earth bodies worn out, it is time for our spirit or energy to return back to the Source. This is how I explain the death of a loved one to a mourner.

Actually, during our earthly lives, we should attempt to remain connected to this flow. Alienation, depression, greed, corruption, and the like happen if we become disconnected.

Many religions acknowledge this great Oneness. In the Jewish tradition, the main prayer is the Shema, and it ends with "the Lord is One." Many say this prayer is a statement of monotheism, but certainly early Hebrews would have said, "There is only one God." In my way of thinking, by saying, "the Lord is One," they were telling us that everything is interconnected in the Oneness of the divine. It is from this prayer that I came to my belief about the non-duality of the Universe. It is not God versus humans. God is within us and we are part of "Godness." It's all one.

This is a very simple philosophy. Yet when you truly feel it, you understand how powerful it is, and you understand the meaning of life.

The Sanskrit word *namaste* teaches us one way to practice this belief. It means "the divine within me recognizes and honors the divine within you." What if every person on this planet really understood and practiced this? Can you imagine the power of love and respect that would lift us up and encircle the planet? If we are all One and created out of the same stuff — why do we hate? How can we even hate ourselves if we come from this glorious source of energy?

If we find ourselves disconnected, alienated, alone, or even just grumpy, what are we to do? How are we to get reconnected to the divine flow?

The first thing we must do is make atonement. Not atonement for our sins, but for being disconnected from the Source. I think the only sin is not to realize the power and the grandeur of this interconnectedness and not to value the life-giving and sustaining energy. When I think of atonement, I think of it as at-one-ment. We must become One again.

I imagine that you are probably thinking, "Oh sure, easier said than done," and I agree with you. But it is also something we all have the power to do if we practice it until it becomes part of our nature.

Savoring the Perfect Omelet

Let me share with you some of my practice tips for when I find myself disconnected from this divine Source.

1. Step outside. Certainly God is everywhere, but sometimes we forget. Stepping outside into nature is one sure way to get "God-smacked" into seeing the incredible beauty and power of the divine. Even if I find myself in a concrete jungle, I look for life. I may see a bird fly by, or a tiny flower growing up through the asphalt. Connect with life, breathe it in, and know that you, too, have this strength, beauty, and power.

2. The biggest re-connector for me, because I am painfully shy, is to

greet every person I meet during a day. Sure, many will walk right by me, but I connect with enough people to bring me back into connection with the Source and, I hope, to help them connect, too.

3. Spend time with animals. Adopt a rescue pet. Look into their eyes and know you are connected. Let them teach you how to love unconditionally.

4. Listen. Listen to the quiet. Listen to the sounds of nature. Listen, truly listen, when someone is talking to you.

5. Sit in meditation or prayer and breathe in divine energy or spirit. Let it fill your soul.

6. Look at challenges, obstacles, and heartbreaks as life's teachers. Learn from them. Find the silver lining in every cloud.

7. Do random acts of kindness. I actually tithe to the planet. I set aside about 10 percent of my money and instead of giving it to a house of worship, I return it to the Source. I see far more benefit from this practice than I ever did with traditional tithing. I will randomly give my co-workers a gift card for a cup of coffee or tea, donate a small amount to an animal rescue group, or bake a treat and take it into an office. Hand out money to homeless people. Bring flowers to a neighbor. Send a card for no particular reason. There are so many small gestures we can do each day to stay connected, and I promise that by doing them, we re-energize our own happiness.

8. Last, practice the smaller "ones" such as one breath, one moment, one day. Live in the moment. Know that every breath we take is a gift; every sunrise and sunset a blessing.

9. Never waste your time or become complacent. Practice goodness and "Godness" – living in the One: one breath, one

kind act, one hug, one love — to attain inner and outer peace. Use the healing of your brokenness to connect to the Source, making not only the perfect omelet, but an awesome life.

Rabbi Ann White, JD, is calm amid chaos. As a trauma chaplain at a busy trauma center, Ann turned to chaplaincy as a way to bring peace into troubled hearts, including her own. She is the author of *Living with Spirit Energy* and *The Sacred Art of Dog Walking: Making the Ordinary Extraordinary*. She also hosts a weekly radio show on BlogTalkRadio. com called "Creating Calm within Chaos." You can reach her at www. CreatingCalmWithinChaos.com.

Turning Your Personal Challenge into a Gift That Keeps On Giving

Arielle Ford

I HAD A HISTORY OF WHAT I CALL dating "supertoads." These weren't mere pond frogs; they were beyond that, and they all had a pattern. They were mostly type A, alpha males, narcissistic, commitment-phobic, and detached. I'd be in a relationship with them for a year or two, but it was always all about them. I would constantly try to change, control, and manipulate them in order to be happy.

Then one day, at the age of forty-three, I woke up and had this sort of epiphany, like, "Oh my God! What have I been doing? I'm such a great manifester when it comes to money, career, travel, and where to live, but I'm just so lame in the area of relationships. What do I need to do? What do I need to change?"

A couple of things came about. One, I realized that everything I was accusing these guys of being... were really *my* issues. I had been in therapy before, so I decided to go back and really work on my own intimacy and commitment challenges. I knew I needed to clear whatever emotional blocks I still had if I was to ever attract the man of my dreams. I also started to create some forgiveness processes to do. I wanted to forgive myself for all the ways I'd judged myself for having made mistakes in relationships, and I had a short list of guys I needed to forgive as well, as I had been holding thoughts of them having done me wrong. I started to really do a deep inquiry with myself to discover the truth about the kind of relationship that would contribute to my long-term happiness. What would that relationship feel like? What were the heart traits and qualities this person would possess?

Secondly, I also wanted to see if all the manifestation tools and techniques that I had used since I had first learned them in 1984 would work in the area of romance. I really had no idea if it would work, but I had collected a wide array of prayers, rituals, processes, projects, incantations, and affirmations — things that I had used successfully in other areas of my life to attract the results I desired. So I made a list of what I wanted in a perfect partner. The trouble was it was way too long. I decided to start organizing it to determine what I would need to do by prioritizing my "must haves" to manifest a soul mate.

While I had been looking to date rock stars (not musical rock stars, but business rock stars and high-performance kinds of guys) what I really discovered that I most desired was to be with somebody for whom I would be the center of their Universe. I wanted them to have that generosity of spirit to give me the time, energy, and attention that I really craved. I also was smart enough to know that my ideal soul mate would not be the CEO of a Fortune 100 company, as they most likely needed to be the center of attention and wouldn't have time to dedicate to me. What I did know was how I wanted to feel. I wanted to be able to wake up in the morning knowing and feeling that I was loved. I wanted somebody who was generous with their time and affection – somebody who was clear that the greatest part of their day was spending time with me.

The relationships I'd experienced up to this point had been very painful, which left me in a state of yearning and disappointment. I'd had enough of being on the sidelines waiting for crumbs. "When is it my turn?" became my constant question.

All through this period I'd built this amazing career as a successful publicist. I was so comfortable being behind the scenes that it took a long time for me to even be willing to come out of the shadows.

One day I had this real "aha!" moment. I had just gotten out of another messy relationship when my assistant said to me, "Trying to get 'John' to love you is like asking a man with no arms to hold you." I thought, "Oh my God! She's so right! It's not even his fault. He doesn't have the capacity to love me. It's not possible. It's just who he is." That's when I really started to see that I had this pattern of choosing the wrong person over and over again. I made the decision right there and then that I'd rather be alone than to continually keep making these same mistakes.

So I took time for myself and focused on creating a "wish list" of the heart traits and qualities I wanted my soul mate to possess. This was not a list containing physical traits I desired such as "He needs to be 6'2", 180 pounds," etc., although I believe it's okay to include a few of these characteristics. However, I don't believe any of those things contribute to your long-term happiness, which is really what you're designing here. The one physical quality I did write down was that he be someone with grey hair because every time I envisioned my soul mate, that was what I saw.

After sorting out my priorities, I then created a ritual to release it to the Universe. As I'm a big fan of the lunar cycle, I decided to let go of my list on a Friday when there was a new moon. Fridays are the day of Venus, the goddess of love and beauty, so that became the day I released my list to the world.

I took my beautiful piece of stationery with my list on it down to the ocean. I read through it a final time and said a prayer of deep gratitude, thanking the Universe for delivering to me my perfect right partner. I then burned it and scattered the ashes into the water. Afterwards I took myself out to lunch, ordered a glass of champagne, and made a silent toast to my soul mate while saying, "Well, wherever you are right now, I just want you to know the cosmic welcome mat is out."

Those were the first couple of steps that I took, but there were many, many more. I feng shui-ed my house, created a relationship corner, and made a treasure map/vision board. I cut the energetic cords between me and my past lovers, and cleaned out the energy throughout my home of past guys who had been there. I opened and made space in my closet, chest of drawers, and the nightstand. I did what I call "feathering the nest." I also prepared myself to receive my soul mate in body, mind, spirit, energetically, psychically, every which way you can imagine, and within six months I met my wonderful husband-to-be. We ended up meeting through business, and within three weeks of our first date we got engaged, and a year later we had not one, but three weddings!

The first wedding was blessed by an Indian holy woman named Amma. It was a Hindu ceremony, so it wasn't legal in the US. The second wedding was a very traditional kind of wedding ceremony. The only thing that was untraditional was that Kenny Loggins was both our wedding singer and the minister. Then we had a third ceremony on top of a mountain that consisted of a pagan handfasting. I guess you have to wait until you're forty-four to experience three wonderful and distinct ceremonies!

You know, I have so much evidence that it's absolutely possible to create magic in your life. And what it takes is four things: time, energy, intention, and attention. You really have to be committed to it. There are a lot of people out there who say, "Oh, I'd really like to be with my soul mate, but…" and that's where everything goes crazy for them, because they are hanging on to these misbegotten beliefs that they're too old, too fat, too damaged, all the good mates are taken, they're unworthy of love, and it's never going to happen for them.

When trying to attract your soul mate, it's really people's beliefs that get in the way. I know this was true for me. And we all have a choice in what we believe. The thing that a lot of people don't understand is something that I call "emotional maturity." When we're emotionally mature adults, we manage our thoughts and emotions. We don't allow our thoughts and emotions to manage us. So what that means is if a thought comes up – "Oh, I'm just too old" – then the adult part of us says, "That's just not true." If we're overtaken by a wave of emotion, the adult part of us says, "Okay, let me experience this. What am I feeling? Is there any truth to it? And what can I do to release the feeling?" Positive, action-oriented people don't get run over by negativity and thoughts.

Thankfully there's an abundance of resources to help you manage your emotions and learn to let them go. (Just look on the internet for EFT, Sedona Method, HeartMath, etc. to find some tools.) And if you need more help, I highly recommend working with a coach or therapist.

Probably the most important part of attracting your soul mate is about believing – knowing that you deserve to be happy and you deserve to be loved. My grandmother always said, "There's a lid for every pot," that there's somebody out there for you… and it's important to believe this in your search for lasting love.

And here's the evidence for that. Right now there are close to seven billion people alive on the planet. Half of them are single. Statistically, the odds are in your favor that there are multiple possible partners for you. And there was another statistician who ran some numbers who said that every individual has more than a million potential soul mates walking the planet right now. So you can hang on to the theory that it's too late, all the good ones are taken, there's no one out there for you, or you can choose to disbelieve your wrong thinking and choose to believe what the statistics state – that there are plenty of potential partners out there for you.

If you had told me seven years ago, "Oh, you're going to have this bestselling book and you're going to be teaching workshops about love and relationships," I would have said, "You are completely crazy!" because it just wasn't on my radar at all. And, yet, now that I'm doing it, I feel so blessed and fortunate, because there's nothing more fun than talking about love all the time!

Seeing what's possible, and being able to witness that my theory works for thousands of people, confirms that I didn't just get "lucky." I tapped in to some basic universal laws that I was fortunate to have learned and used in other areas of my life, but the most basic part of it is this: If you can get clear on what your intention is – what you most desire – and then you can feel in every cell of your body that what you're asking for is already yours and on some dimension you already have this, then it's coming to you. You cannot not get it. And it takes practice. It's like a muscle. You don't expect to run a marathon the first time you put on your sneakers.

So the next time you catch yourself thinking, "I'm never going to find happiness and love," stop and reverse what you're saying to: "I can see myself happy, in love, and content." Drop the negativity and put the universal "Law of Attraction" into action.

It works every time.

Arielle Ford is a gifted writer and the author of eight books including the international bestseller, *The Soulmate Secret: Manifest the Love of Your Life with the Law of Attraction*. She has been called "The Cupid of Consciousness" and "The Fairy Godmother of Love." She lives in La Jolla, California, with her husband/soul mate, Brian Hilliard, and their feline friends. Visit www.ArielleFord.com, www.SoulmateSecret.com, or www.WabiSabiLove.com.

Never Give Up! Keep the Vision

Betty Marchorro

IMMENSELY GRATEFUL I AM FOR THE GIFT of being able to breathe on Planet Earth at this magnificent time. Hard, painful, and lonely has been the journey that I have had to travel to arrive at this moment. I now know there is a reason for everything we experience, even if we don't understand it.

I was born with a hunger for knowledge and understanding of life, in a tiny village in the eastern region of Guatemala. At the time of my early life, it was hard to think of sending children to school, especially if those children were girls. We didn't have a school, and we were very isolated from the rest of society.

It was beautiful to live surrounded by giant, majestic trees, sharing our space with domestic and wild animals, eating fresh harvest from the fields, and being able to contemplate the brightest sky I have ever seen. We didn't have electricity, therefore we could better appreciate the light from above.

My mom says that I was always asking adults to write letters on paper as I wanted to draw them. She had been taught the basics of reading and writing, so when I was about to turn seven, given my eagerness to learn, she decided to teach me what she knew.

She was amazed at how fast and easily I learned. She tells me she didn't have to repeat the lessons in order for me to grasp the meaning. When my dad realized I was a fast learner, he began to teach me as well. He had taught himself to read, write, and do basic math. He had never attended school. He was surprised as well at my capacity for learning, and he told my mom that I should go to school.

Even though my mom had a lot of work to do, taking care of my three younger sisters and me, doing all the housework, making lunch and taking it to the fields for my dad and other farmers who worked with him, she took me to and from school, which was about two and a half miles away, every day. I have always been grateful and filled with admiration for everything she has done, never complaining, or even mentioning it.

When I got to school, I was so excited to learn about new things, but this excitement didn't last long. Instead of learning new things, I felt I was going backwards; I was being taught dots and lines! I felt so sad and frustrated. When I told my mom I wasn't taught new things, she said that perhaps the next day would bring new lessons. I kept waiting, but it turned out to be a long one as things didn't change much. I became bored and frustrated. I did everything the teacher asked, as I didn't seem to have any other choice.

After realizing that things wouldn't change, I decided to start reading books on my own, but I was always ahead of my classmates. I got along with everyone, but it was very hard for me to make close friends. I felt I didn't have a place in the world. The other children looked at me with a mixture of admiration and rejection. I became a very miserable and isolated child. I had only one friend in the classroom, and she was four years older than I. She stood up for me when other children wanted to beat me up in any way she was aware of.

I was always passionate about singing, writing, and acting, but the sadness I started to accumulate inside my heart also made me repress all of those gifts that I had inside. I was overweight, and my peers called me ugly, degrading, and humiliating names. I felt painfully rejected, and so I learned to reject myself.

Since I was a lonely child, I found solace in writing. Pen and paper were my friends, but I wasn't supported in my writing efforts. One day when I was in second grade, my teacher asked us to write a composition for Mother's Day. Very excited, I did mine and when I gave it to the teacher, the principal who was standing next to her, asked to see it. After reading it, she asked me from where I had taken it. When I told her that I had written it, she said I must have copied it from a book, as it was too good to have been written by me. It was a contest and she took my composition out of it. I don't remember, but one of my aunts says that she recalls that I cried a lot because of this rejection.

All my years at elementary school were the same, with the exception of fourth grade. During that year I felt I was learning at least new things in math. My teacher wanted to push me ahead to the fifth grade, but the principal said the system didn't allow it.

My other oasis in the desert I was living, beside the love and care of my mom, was our small old radio on which I listened to children's stories every day. I learned to awaken my imagination and draw mental images from the stories I heard. These fed my faith and belief in dreams and the power of our thoughts and visions. I don't know if I used to believe in actual fairies, but I believed there is a magical power inside the human being. I also kept writing, but never showed any of my writings to anybody until I got to high school.

When I began junior high school, we left the village and moved to town. It was the same sad story at school, and in my experience every day seemed to get worse. I was crying all the time, and again, I was unable to make close friends. By this time I had developed eating disorders from bulimia to anorexia, acne problems, and suffered from depression, asthma, and anxiety attacks.

It seems I was always a natural counselor. People came to me for advice, but I felt nobody could understand me. I always wanted to help people ease their pain, but I didn't know how to ease mine.

In senior high school, a teacher quit because he couldn't answer my questions, and another teacher asked me very often if what he was teaching was right. It was so frustrating that I think I gave up on school. I continued going only because I didn't see any other option.

My eating disorders worsened. I would go days without food and then stuff myself compulsively. Depression got so deep that there were days where I could hardly open my eyes. My mom took me to the doctor, who sent me to see a psychiatrist. He put me on antidepressants, and I had some sessions with him. I didn't understand why I had to take them to alleviate my emotional pain, and hated being dependent on a pill to keep me whole.

I started an intensive inner healing on myself, first in a prayer group, then with self-help books and courses, meditation, visualization, relaxation techniques, and healers. I read every book I could find on forgiveness and inner healing.

I had to learn that I am not a victim, that even though I might not be able to see, that I always have a choice. I had to learn that happiness is a choice and not something that comes in a package that we can get from someone or somewhere. I had to learn that I can choose my thoughts, and thus my emotions, and create my reality. I had to learn that if things don't seem to be happening, I can co-create them with the Divine, and many times I need to remind myself to never give up and always keep going, no matter what.

In 1993, I got a scholarship from the US government to study there. I graduated in 1995, getting an Associate Degree in small business management and a Certificate in bilingual marketing at Edmonds Community College in Lynnwood, Washington. While I was there, I kept taking therapies for my own healing and learning about other modalities. When I returned to Guatemala after two years of study, I opened an alternative therapies clinic in my hometown, Asuncion Mita, where I have worked on physical and emotional healing. Throughout all these changes and healing, I still longed to sing and write.

Finally, in 2008, I recorded my first CD with ten of my own compositions, and now I sing professionally and write about my experiences. I have had the opportunity to travel, maybe not completely around the world yet, but I have enjoyed many trips to different places in the US, Europe, Central America, the Caribbean, and Egypt, to name a few. The most important thing is now my heart feels lighter and lighter every day, and I am grateful for every experience, every tear, every rejection, and for the courage to keep going. I thank the little girl inside of me who kept believing and visualizing herself free and happy.

It has been a long journey, but now I can speak of it all with an open heart and without the emotional attachment that I used to in the past. Along the journey I learned to heal myself and help others do the same, and it's a joy to share my story with the world. In my clinic I do therapies to heal physical and emotional pain and improve the person's general well-being.

After having healed herself from the emotional pain causing her depression, eating disorders, asthma, and anxiety attacks, Betty Marchorro now helps to heal others. She specializes in relaxation and inner healing techniques, and gives private sessions and talks. She especially loves inner-child healing. A lover of words and music, she's also a singer and writer who composes and performs her own songs. You can contact her at BettyMarchorro@gmail.com or by phone at (502) 40421171.

The Fat Lady Sings

Carol C. Hess

"CAROL, YOU HAVE A RELATIVELY RARE and very aggressive form of breast cancer." Had I heard right? One look at my friend Paula's uncharacteristically solemn face, and I had my answer.

The breast surgeon continued with more facts, figures, and information. I had to keep asking her to repeat herself. She was patient with me, and I could tell she wasn't the patient type. That patience scared the hell out of me.

"Sorry," I apologized. "I normally grasp things quickly, don't I, Paula?"

Paula looked startled and nodded. Her eyes slid away from mine.

A couple of days later I was more myself with the oncologist. This time I was absorbing the vast amount of information being delivered. My friend Wendy, who had insisted on coming with me to this appointment, was taking copious notes and asking lots of questions.

I didn't have any questions. I knew everything I needed to know. I was in trouble – big trouble. The oncologist wouldn't give me survival statistics, claiming it was pointless until after the surgery. Fair enough. But her demeanor and the tone of her voice, to say nothing of the concerned expression in her eyes, weren't reassuring.

Several hours after Wendy dropped me off at home, it hit me. I was going to die. Soon.

I looked out the window at the bleak winter landscape of January in Maine. I drew the curtains and turned on all the lights against the encroaching dark that always falls so early at that time of year. For the umpteenth time, I thought, "I can't wait until the days are longer."

And then I fell into hell. And I stayed there for three days and three nights. I had just run out of time. All those things I was going to do – lose weight, get into shape, become a better person – they weren't going to happen. The life partner I was going to find, the book I was going to write, the dream business I was going to launch, the dream house I was going to build – they weren't going to happen either.

My death would cause barely a ripple on anyone's pond. A few people would be sad for a short period of time, and then I would be forgotten. I was leaving no legacy behind to let the world know I had existed. Most people at least have the legacy of their children. I didn't even have that.

I had created nothing – no partnership, no children, no book, no business, no house – nothing. My life, my existence on the planet, had counted for nothing. I had really blown it.

For years I had postponed really living my life, and now my life, such as it was in all its smallness, was going to end soon. I was going to die, never having done what I wanted to do, never having become who I knew I could be.

Why?

Because I was fat.

I had decided I wouldn't really start to live until I got thin. I didn't really deserve a great life until I got thin. I couldn't really be happy until I got thin. Only something had gone horribly wrong. I had never gotten thin, and now I was going to die before I had lived.

The despair I felt was profound, heavy, all encompassing. I dropped into a deep, dark abyss from which there was no escape, and I stayed there for three long days and three even longer nights.

Here's an entry from my journal during that time:

"I feel an aloneness so profound it flows into and echoes in every cavity of my body and every crevice of my mind. I know this feeling. It's where I've lived for far too long. I used to drink to avoid feeling this place, but the booze stopped working. So then I ate to numb the feeling. But that stopped working too. My aloneness just got worse. Yesterday I was diagnosed with breast cancer, and it doesn't sound good. My hope that someday my life would get better, that someday I would get better, just got ripped away from me.

And now I'm staring into a dark corridor of fear that goes on forever. Fear that I will die the way I have lived – abandoned and alone. Fear that I have wasted my precious one and only life. Fear that I have counted for nothing, that I have made no difference."

Then something shifted. I woke up the morning of the fourth day with the firm resolve that I wasn't going to die the same way I had lived. I wasn't going out full of anger, self-pity, and resentment, with my head bowed in defeat because I had failed Life 101. I was going out with my head held high and my heart full of love and compassion for everyone, especially for myself. I couldn't make up for all those wasted years, but I could live my last weeks as consciously and spiritually as possible.

Then I put in a phone call to my oncologist, Sarah. I had a few follow-up questions for her. As I started to ask my third question, Sarah interrupted me.

"Carol, I want to emphasize that your cancer is curable."

"Huh? Did you just say my cancer is curable?"

"Yes."

"Oh."

As low as I had sunk during the time I had spent in the abyss was as high as I now soared. I felt so light and free. I wouldn't have been surprised if I had started levitating. I still didn't know how much time I had left, and wouldn't know until after the surgery and all the test results, but I did know there was a good chance my life wasn't about to end after all. And that chance was enough for now. More than enough.

I wonder if my resolve to live consciously and spiritually in the time left to me had anything to do with what still feels like the miracle of my reprieve. Did I unknowingly make a deal with my Higher Power? "I'll live consciously and spiritually if You'll just give me some more time to live."

That doesn't really sound like me. I'm not much of a haggler. Just ask the African vendors who loved doing business with the white memsahib who didn't bargain over prices. It's not my nature to negotiate with the Divine. Right or wrong, I've got more of a "thank you very much" or "shake my fist at the sky" kind of relationship with my Higher Power.

In any case, a reprieve is certainly what I received that day and continue to receive. I'm cancer-free today and have an excellent chance of remaining that way. If I did indeed strike a deal with the Powers That Be, then I did a damned good job of it. Although I've got to admit that keeping my end of the bargain, living consciously and spiritually, isn't the easiest thing I've ever done. But it's taught me something really important.

I'm a star. And I'm going to allow myself to shine. I'm stopping my hugging the walls and staying in the shadows act because I'm fat. I'm stepping into the center of the room so you can see my light.

I'm not going to be that fat woman with her nose pressed up against the cold window, looking at the warm party going on inside.

I'm going to be that fat woman who is slinging wide open the door to that party and striding inside with her head held high.

I'm turning the key in the lock of the prison cell I sentenced myself to because I was fat. I'm setting myself free. And I'm not "weighting" one more day, one more hour, one more minute to do it.

Today is the day *The Fat Lady Sings*, but it sure as hell ain't over. It's just beginning.

Carol Hess is a writer, survivor, blogger, cat lover, coach, and star polisher. She works with overweight women, helping them discover and polish their stars. This is an excerpt from her book, *The Fat Lady Sings*. You can read her blog, purchase her book, and find out more about her services at www.StarPolisher.com.

Finding Forgiveness

Carolyn Hidalgo, CPCC, ACC

DO YOU STRUGGLE WITH A PAST disappointment or the weight of resentment from a broken trust? I've resisted forgiveness, feeling like I'm condoning something wrong or allowing others not to take responsibility for unacceptable behavior. These false beliefs kept me trapped under the weight of un-forgiveness. I discovered that achieving forgiveness brought an unexpected gift: strength and inner trust that allows life to flow and my authentic self to shine. Being with your own vulnerability in any situation calling for forgiveness is where your true power lies. It opens a space to see yourself with more clarity, and discover a timeless wisdom…

"There is no right or wrong, but thinking makes it so." — Shakespeare

When I choose to believe "I am right, and you are wrong," I feel a need to correct, control, convince, or change you (the 4 Cs, as I call them). I subconsciously create the energy of self-righteousness: "I am superior and you are inferior." Blaming and complaining gives away my power by choosing to react with "You are the cause of my experience," or the victim mentality. A higher level of consciousness recognizes that in judging others, I create my own suffering. I become attached to "being right" and lose my sense of compassion and understanding.

"We don't receive wisdom; we must discover it for ourselves after a journey that no one can take for us or spare us." — Marcel Proust

We label words and actions of others that have destructive or harmful consequences as "wrong," but something self-destructive happens when we think of someone "being wrong." We now see another human being as the destructive energy for the things they say and do. People become objects or problems that need to be fixed. We criticize and judge, creating a reaction of defensiveness such as, "How could you think such a thing?" or resistance, "What you believe is not true!" Tension or conflict erupts. How often do you resonate with well-meaning "advice" people think you need to hear, believing they are "right?"

When you release the right/wrong mindset, energetically you are shifting away from your ego's fear-based need to "be right" and towards your higher vibration of love, where curiosity, understanding, and compassion are available. Compassion differs from feeling sorry for someone, which is disempowering. When you jump into "helping," where pity is the driver, you stay stuck and become the enabler for someone else's suffering. Compassion sees everyone as equal, uplifting the human spirit.

"We see the world, not as it is, but as we are — or, as we are conditioned to see it."
— Stephen Covey, The 7 Habits of Highly Effective People

What is it about things people say and do that are hurtful? What others say and do is a reflection of their reality. You can only do your "best" in any given moment. Someone's "best" may not look anything like your "best," which develops over time from your social upbringing, beliefs, knowledge, experiences, and genetics. The moment you release your criticism and judgment, you allow others to be who they are, walk their own path, make their own mistakes, and ultimately grow spiritually.

Those who throw the first stone and justify it suffer blindly. People are only capable of taking responsibility for what they say and do based on their perspective, which is limited to what they see, but we expect others to take responsibility for what we see.

"I know you think you understand what you thought I said, but I'm not sure you realize that what you heard is not what I meant."
— *Alan Greenspan*

It's difficult not to feel compassion for those who are self-destructive, and reach for the empowering choice to "forgive others for they know not what they do." (Luke 23:34.) Yet this is the practice of compassion that returns you back to the love within yourself.

When someone's energy is destructive, you must walk away for your own well-being. Distancing yourself from energy that drains you strengthens you in two ways: You attract higher-energy people who nourish and support your best self, and by wishing others well on their journey (forgiveness), you build a deeper inner trust. Any difficult experience becomes a gift for your own growth.

"Trust yourself, then you will know how to live." — Goethe

Imagine someone who has lost your trust, and notice which of the five thought patterns and corresponding emotions you normally choose. Is it a pleasant feeling like peace and understanding, or difficult, like frustration and resentment?

1. HAVING AN OPINION – "I think you are untrustworthy. I understand this is not a fact, just my thoughts. You are free to think otherwise." We are each entitled to our own opinions.

2. HOLDING A BELIEF – "I believe you are untrustworthy. I won't likely believe the contrary unless you provide me with extraordinary proof." Beliefs are not facts, but have developed over time and are less subject to change.

3. DISCERNMENT – "From my firsthand experience of hearing you say one thing and doing another, and confirming evidence, I discern you are someone who is untrustworthy." I may need to walk away because trust is a value in my relationships. I don't condemn you because I understand you are simply living your reality.

4. CRITICISM – "You are untrustworthy and should stop saying one thing and doing another. You are wrong and no one will trust you. You will lose all your friends." You feel a need to correct, control, convince, or change someone's thinking to be your right way.

5. JUDGMENT – "Because you are untrustworthy, you are bad, selfish, or mean, and should be punished to learn your lesson. You don't deserve any friends." Judgment is criticism taken up a notch where you stand in a superior place looking down upon someone, which can lead to hatred, resentment, and contempt.

Notice when you say or think the word "should" in relation to someone. "You should…" projects your "right" way of seeing the world onto someone who is simply living their reality. Practice letting go of "should," and notice what happens within.

How can you tell the difference between criticizing and judging versus having an opinion?

If you think someone is lazy or stupid, you may believe this as having an opinion, but would you call yourself these words proudly? Certain words hold a negative vibe that condemns. Let go of making someone "wrong"; "lazy" becomes someone unproductive by your standards; "stupid" may be someone lacking the ability to process mentally as you do. We compare and compete with our version of "right." Sure there are better ways of doing things that lead to achieving higher outcomes, and people with more knowledge and mental abilities, but no person is better or worse than another.

"The pendulum of the mind oscillates between sense and nonsense, not between right and wrong." — Carl Jung

Each of us is on a spiritual path, evolving with our own life experience. Who am I to step on your path with my criticism and judgment? We can teach, model, lend support, positively influence, seek to understand, share, and speak our truth to those ready to hear. Values of safety, freedom, and harmony must be protected when interacting with someone who has lost their way or requires guidance because of their age or experience. In judging others we condemn ourselves, for we are all ONE — what you do unto others, you do to yourself.

We ultimately want the same experience: to be seen, heard, and loved unconditionally for who we are. Do you see and hear others transparently?

The Steps to Achieving Forgiveness

1. SEE. See when you are criticizing or judging someone, making them wrong with your need to control, correct, convince, or change others (the 4 Cs). Notice any false beliefs that hold you back from forgiving.

2. OWN. Take ownership and responsibility for your part in blaming and complaining, no matter what someone's said or done. Stop comparing and competing with others — each of us is unique. Shift to cooperation and understanding.

3. SURRENDER. Let go of your attachment to "being right" by releasing your own energy of criticism and judgment. Your disappointment, anger, and resentment will fade.

4. SHARE. Communicate your new awareness either to the person you need to forgive or to someone you trust. Distinguish the words and actions that cross your values from a person's spirit. Are someone's choices constructive (loving) or destructive (unloving)?

5. COMPASSION. Practice being compassionate by understanding that someone else's perspective is different from our own, and knowing we are each doing our best with our free will. Be curious, and open.

One final note: Self-criticism and self-judgment brings feelings of guilt, unworthiness, and not feeling "good enough." Treating yourself with compassion is the gift of non-judgment you can give yourself.

You have achieved forgiveness when you feel the inner peace of experiencing the light of "God" in everyone, including yourself, no matter what was said or done, and in the process you will have learned to let go of judgment...

"There is a field beyond right and wrong. I will meet you there."
— Rumi

Carolyn Hidalgo, CPCC, ACC, is a relationship coach committed to transforming her clients' relationships into more fulfilling, authentic connections. She teaches a practice of non-judgment and compassion that allows love to flow more naturally. Carolyn was trained through the Coaches Training Institute, and holds a specialist degree in cognitive psychology from the University of Toronto. Visit www.Carolyn-Hidalgo.com to get your copy of her FREE "Relationship Report" to minimize conflicts, achieve forgiveness, and deepen love.

Spiritwise

Carolyn Rose Hart, MEd.

HOW WAS IT THAT I BECAME enmeshed in the so-called American Dream – a dream of overconsumption – without regard for my fellow human beings? I was truly in the throes of acquiring every convenience and new technology that would make my life "sweet." In doing so, I remained so busy that I was no longer a soul having a human experience. I was a do it, get it done, and achieve it kind of gal.

Two years into retirement, I became aware that things were not making me happy. I was really a human being with a deep yearning to connect with other human beings, and had not been aware of this fact. This yearning was calling me, NOW. I decided to listen to this calling to connect with other cultures and other human beings who live lives much different from my own.

So in 2006, I sold my 2,500 square-foot home and most of the trappings I had collected over twenty-five years. The remainder went into a storage unit or into my car. I began driving across the United States, knowing the journey would last at least one year. However, the exquisiteness of the human connections and adventure provided me with the wherewithal to continue traveling for three additional years.

The majority of my four years of travel was spent in the western United States, Uganda, Bali, Brazil, and Ecuador. I immersed myself with the locals by living in their homes or in close proximity. This broad range of travel, coupled with my previous travels to many European countries, provided a reframing of my basic assumptions that my country is the best country in the world, people everywhere are different, and environmental and social justice issues exist in only a few countries around the world.

Those four years of travel opened my eyes to what is true about the world and what is true about how I was existing with my fellow human beings. It became clear that people can be happy living their entire life in one country, as the Balinese do, never leaving to explore the world. Their home is the world to them, and they cherish family as everything.

There are cultures around the world such as the Achuar in Ecuador who are protecting Mother Nature and walking a sacred path upon her surface, keepers of the rainforest. They live sustainably in a community in which needs and wants are met through sharing. They only take what they need, and always give back to the earth, thus balancing the ecosystem. I am forever grateful for their presence at this time in history.

Unexamined assumptions, which are beliefs personally acquired without questioning, became a new idea for me. As my previous life revolved around a culture of competition, acquisition, and a belief that science will solve all the problems of the world, I immersed myself in these beliefs, never questioning what was really so. I was sucked into the group energy, believing that humans are masters over nature. Such unexamined assumptions set up a pattern of taking what we want from the world because we have worked hard and believe that we deserve to have things that make us happy. This seemed to have become part of my DNA. I really bought into a logic that helped me to stay in the space of feeling I could have it all, and if I had it all, I would be happy. I was reeled in like a fishing line.

While in Uganda with my friend Jo and her non-profit company, Partnering for Africa's Future, I was appalled that teachers in many village schools did not have any college education. Thus, I initiated the Uganda Teacher Fund, sending teachers to school during their breaks. The program required these teachers to share their new knowledge and skills with fellow teachers upon return to their school. When the funding dried up, they found ways to continue the program, and with head teacher Edith's support, they expanded the program, increasing the quality of the school. The school went from 107 students in 2005 to 409 students in 2011. They had all their own answers and did not need an American to come tell them how to do it. Wahoo! Another burst unexamined assumption.

As I traveled, my eyes were opened and I awakened. I began to see how plundered the environment is, and that social justice issues are everywhere on this planet. I began to see that there is another way to be, and it was forming before my eyes. It is the "New Paradigm" that is surfacing in every country of the world. There is another way to be that encourages us to be more respectful of our fellow human beings and more respectful of Mother Earth.

We are all connected. We are all one. There is no separation between ourselves, other life forms, or any one of our seven billion brothers and sisters on earth. We all want love, safety, our physical needs met, and connection. A "New Great Story" is forming, and we are all in this together.

What comes up for me is a perfect storm allowing a treasure trove of solutions to show up and be a powerful force for change. We are living in exciting times and we are all being called to greatness. We can choose to be inspired and choose a new way to be as a species... and we already are.

My unexamined assumptions are being forever scrutinized now. I have learned to constantly stay in the space of the unknown, and one of questioning what I think I know and believe. I have learned to use what I already own before buying something new. I am amazed at how many different objects can be used for things they were not intended for. I am also amazed at how little I actually need in order to be happy.

As I focus on what really matters to me, other human beings, I begin to see inspiration from other people, and that all beings deserve to be treated with dignity and respect. My basic assumptions were barriers, and I know they will continue to rear their ugly heads. However, when they do, I thank them, remember who I am, and what my gifts to the world are.

Becoming clear about my personal gifts occurred through my four years of travel. I was blessed with being able to explore healing through Gestalt therapy and private counseling with an exquisite therapist. As a result of the therapy and counseling, I have cleared past pain from an abusive, dysfunctional childhood. Assisting with this process was dance, massage, drumming, chanting, meditation, journaling, and many other modalities that crossed my path. Each person benefits from their own modality avenue. Doing individual work is crucial for stepping up to our collective journey at this time in history.

It was no accident that I spent my life teaching challenged learners. I know that my gift is in teaching, as well as in writing. I have also learned that I am a seed dropper; I start projects and programs, then release them to the newly formed community to name, change, and evolve. I facilitate programs and train others to facilitate programs based on sustainability. I am now coaching others to identify their gifts and step up to sharing them with the world. It doesn't get any better than this.

Today I choose to be a minimalist, living in a 350 square-foot apartment, and I have all I need. I focus on living a life that comes from the heart. I say yes to vulnerability and "allow the winds of life to flow freely over my soul," as Ocean Roberts so eloquently says. I stay open to all the possibilities that come out of my vulnerability.

I have no illusions about the difficulty ahead for all of us, yet I am passionate about this new way to be. I choose to be a catalyst for people doing their individual work to be available for stepping up and being a powerful force for change. If not now... when? Doing our individual work is crucial to showing up in community to make a difference. We have all contributed to what exists in the world today, and it will take all of us to create a new story.

What an incredible opportunity we have as the world evolves. We can choose to have a child sex trade, or we can choose to protect our world's most valuable resource – our children. It is disempowering to say, "Oh, I wish THEY would do something." We can all be agents of change, bringing forth a new, just, and sustainable way to be. In community, we can stand in our power, listen to our souls, find our gifts for the world, and Step Up and Step Out! I would like to acknowledge the wise spirit in all of us. We know what we need to do to make a difference for all life on this planet.

Carolyn is the author of *"Step Up, Step Out - Share Your Gifts and Be an Agent for Change."* In addition, she is a life transition coach and workshop facilitator supporting others to identify and step up to share their gifts. Carolyn trains others to facilitate the Awakening the Dreamer Symposium and Getting Into Action Workshop. Her love of photography and connecting with other life beings is integrated into her writings and teachings. Visit www.CarolynRoseHart.com for your free gift.

Creative Power: Putting Passion into Action

Cassandra Russell

ARE YOU READY TO EMBRACE YOUR power to create a notable life? The time for designing a new lifestyle beckons, urging new ideas. Sitting on the cusp of consciousness allows you to open up to see new starting points.

You may be living in a daily clutter cloud that makes becoming empowered impossible. Creating ways to empower myself has led me to develop my message and has given me a way to create a hopeful intention for empowered living. Igniting creativity is one way I have empowered myself and others. My wish is to help you define what purposeful living means to you. Creating a new empowered lifestyle begins with adding practices that I call "Creative Power Tools."

My Creative Power Journey

My story sheds light on what makes up the background for my own creative power. Creativity runs in my family, as both of my grandmothers were artists, conquering everything from the kitchen to the sewing machine with style and grace. Much of their life's pleasure was generated by their hands. Making something from scratch provided many a worthy challenge for them as they designed their own crafts and clothing. I think their love of hands-on work was passed on to my brother and me. I can also see their talents in my children, which is quite intriguing. My parents, in turn, have manifested their creativity into passions such as gardening and entertaining, to name a few. I have inherited their artistic curiosity as well as their creative expression.

I began my own journey toward creative power at an early age. Feeling like I was a fish out of water could have made me resentful, but it instead made me more sensitive to the feelings of others. Taking pride in my gifts helped my self-esteem and creativity grow. "A unique creative intelligence" became a familiar topic on my report cards. In high school, I read every self-help book that graced my mother's nightstand. My mother was a world issues teacher, so the state of world affairs was a regular topic of debate at our dinner table. My father's generosity was the kindhearted energy in our home. The influence of both my parents, my brother, my aunts, and my teachers made my inner and outer awareness different from that of most teens.

This upbringing led to my choice to go to university in search of meaning and a quest to serve others. I changed my major to philosophy, in which I studied other people's life conclusions. For me this time was like a "brain boot camp" where you had to go to class with an open mind to understand the theories, synthesize them, then write about it later in an exam. This is when I began to first explore my creative mind by learning to look at the duality of life.

My inner transformation continued during my mind-bending academic pursuit at a steady pace until I experienced a devastating time of depression when I was faced with many life choices. I found myself in the depths of despair, desperately trying to make sense of my life.

This was an uphill climb of renewal that triggered a self-directed inner quest. While I felt like I had lost my inner guidance system and woke up crying daily, there was a strength within me that began to emerge. To refocus my mind, I began a red notebook filled with poems and quotes on love to redefine my life. To heal, I reset my resonance with exactly what I thought love was. I did not know about manifesting at the time, but I believe I was defining what I wanted in life by letting the wisdom of other writers move me. Reading this red notebook helped me create a place for the inspiration I needed to raise my vibration. By aligning myself to this vibration of love, I met my husband three months later who provides great encouragement for my creative work.

I was still facing uncertainty about my future when my aunt took me on a healing trip to the Dominican Republic, which was a monumental gesture of kindness to cure my blues. At the time her house was a self-help zone, as her friends had filled her home with inspirational quotes, books, and tapes after her own recovery from breast cancer. I began immersing myself in this sphere of inspiration. Slowly my own philosophy of character building began to grow. I commenced to synthesize ideas from the worlds of self-development and philosophy to create a way to revitalize my power.

Volunteering at the local food bank and other charity work helped me regain the hope to heal. I also volunteered at the campus wellness center where I saw people come in hungry for a context to this stressed-out life we found ourselves in as students. I began to see the value of life in a new way, and became aware that I needed to make choices about my life path. I started to dream about teaching character building to others, but did not yet know how to merge this idea with my creativity.

Reaching Out

At this point, I had two paths in front of me. One that was pre-scribed, and one that meant activating my passion by following my heart toward an artistic life. For me, choosing my own path meant that I had to take a leap of faith, not knowing where it would lead. The courage to make this one decision changed my life and allowed my own creativity to ignite. For the past six years, I have pursued the creative life and an inner quest based on self-development teachings. My son and daughter, husband, loved ones, friends, and readers have all been affected by my passion for living a notable life.

Two years ago, I had a turning point moment when clarity sur-faced and time took on a dream-like quality. I noticed a woman in the car next to mine at the mall crying overwhelmingly. I wished to reach out to her to share words of hope, tales of new horizons, and oppor-tunities for creativity. I also wanted to tell her how interconnected we really are, but most important, that we are never alone. I wanted to knock on the window of politeness that separated us and reach out to her as a fellow human. But where would I begin? Would I have enough time to tell her about her integral part in the magnificence that is all? I desperately wanted to reach out to her. She turned toward me and I gave her a sympathetic smile. My heart broke when her friend ar-rived and the moment to do something was over. It bothered me that I did not have a better way to communicate my concern for her. This is when I realized that I had to put all of my ideas down in a teaching format designed to encourage people. In my mind's eye I pictured that woman and others whom I had been to shy to reach out to, which propelled me to excavate my message. It took courage to open up enough to share my message through my writing and speaking. It was with heartfelt motivation that my words were making a ripple of encouragement to reach people like that woman who was crying in the car that day.

If it had not been for the support of my own loved ones throughout my own time of transformation, I would never have had the courage to reach out to others through my writing. Feeling worthy enough to believe in yourself means acknowledging that there are no guarantees that the choices you make will be right.

Embracing your creative power allows you to explore your nature so you can make reasonable choices that empower those around you. To make a transformative ripple in the world that propels you forward, you can use your creativity to blend your gifts with the hope behind your dreams.

I will leave you with these final words about moving toward living a more fulfilled life: put your passion into action.

Cassandra Russell is an Artist, Author, and Creative Advisor on art and how it empowers people to change their lives for the better. Details about her upcoming book, *Encourage*, and her various workshops can be found on her blog, www.CassandraRussell.typepad.com. Please visit for a complimentary ebook, *How To Start a Simple Art Journaling Practice*.

I Met Death, Divorce, and Cancer... and Then I Met Me

Christine Marmoy

SOMEBODY ONCE TOLD ME, "Christine, the Universe only sends you what you can handle, otherwise it would not." Believe me, when I heard that, my response was quick. "Well, if it is so, maybe it is time for the Universe to know that I'm tired of being able to handle it." Why do we learn, most of the time, through challenges and adversity?

I thought of myself as a free thinker and especially an independent doer, but to a certain level, I was wrong. My experiences colored my actions, and unfortunately, my decisions. For a very long time I thought I could never make the right decisions. All of them ended up putting me in situations I would have rather avoided. So why couldn't I possibly make the right one for a change? The answer to that question is quite simple: The way I was living my life did not allow me to even perceive the right decision. I went through different phases; at times I was living the life I was supposed to based on my education, my environment, and my family. At other times, my life was impregnated with what I thought I wanted as a life, which was, quite frankly, just as bad. Why? Because in each case, I was not being the real me. The worst part was that I had no clue that I was untrue to myself, and later on, once I had realized this, I didn't know how to get in touch with who I really was deep down inside my Soul.

I have had to deal with some major events in my life: death, divorce, and cancer. I knew something had to change, but if only I knew what. Was my ability to make the wrong decision the problem or the symptom? Did I have all this hassle because I had married the wrong man, because I wanted to go to the beach and my boyfriend had drowned, because I had asked to get cancer? Or was it because I was unconsciously pushing myself to the limit to realize who I really was, who I had to become to complete this personal transformation? Like the butterfly emerging from a chrysalis, the old me had to make way for the new, and I was doing a pretty good job at it!

Discovering myself has been, and still is, a work in progress. This process is about allowing yourself to be who you are, and sometimes forcing yourself to do so. As I'm writing this chapter, I have had to go through yet another death. I helped my mom cross over. Now she won't be here anymore to contemplate my achievements, or will she? The last words my mom told me were, "Take my strength." Nice present, but somehow it felt as though if I needed more, it was because more challenges were to be expected.

Would you believe me if I were to tell you that none of this actually helped me find my truth? I discovered myself, my real Self, through my business. How odd is that? Well, not that much as it happens. After talking with many business owners, it seems like our businesses are great teachers, to say the least.

Time and time again I see clients and coaches fighting with the same dilemma, and I'm going to share with you what I tell my clients to help them bring to life their "True Brilliance." This will help you uncover your true Self using your business as your guide.

1. How do you know if you are living true to your Self?

The first step is to be aware that you are untrue to yourself. Easier said than done, I agree. But life itself gives us signs from time to time. They warn us that our way of living is not really the right path for us. I'm sure you've felt that way too. One morning you hate what you are doing and you don't remember why you do what you do. At times it may seem like you are living somebody else's life.

That's what happened to me. I realized that many areas of my life were not satisfactory or fulfilling anymore, even though I had done the same things for more than ten years. So what was happening? Why couldn't I remember the reasons why I was living the way I was? I'm not talking about the "midlife crisis" although it is quite similar from the outside. I'm talking about a deep pain, a profound sadness that you are capable of recognizing now because you've always felt it. You were just so good at numbing the pain until now. However, with time, the suffering becomes unbearable, pushing you to the very edge of what you can humanly handle. The real You claims its spotlight, regardless of whether you want it to or not.

2. What can you do to get in touch with who you truly are?

Once you know that your real you is about to be born, you'll feel the urge to get in touch with it. There are many ways of doing so, many techniques that you may want to consider. Some people like to meditate, others enjoy walking on the beach, yet others need a physical activity. Quite honestly, I cannot recommend one more than the other, for the simple reason that you must find what resonates the most with you. There is no point in wanting to meditate two hours a day if you dislike it, because you will not get the results you want, and you will most likely give up.

Imagine a triangle. On the left corner you have the mind, on the right corner you have the body, and on the top you have the heart. You need to use your mind to direct your thoughts in a way that is beneficial for you. You need to work your body so as to maintain a high level of oxygen, for without this component, the entire machine breaks down. Don't forget that. So why is the heart on the top? Because without love, nothing is really worth the effort! When I put all my love into what I do, life is colorful, life is vibrant, life is joy, and I become all that at the same time.

Now, write in the middle of the triangle the word "Action," because without action, this approach is just a nice idea.

3. How can your business help you become who you truly are?

In business, we like to say that finding that special touch, the unique approach, a different angle, is the key to being successful. However, what I've witnessed is that many wonderful business owners are getting caught up in a web of illusion, in a MUST be different ideology, and so was I.

To be unique, you only need to share your true self. By being true to yourself, you'll allow your Soul to be perceived, and consequently you'll be special. Remember, "Mind over Matter." Now is the time to think, "Heart over Matter," because what you are looking for is waiting for you in your heart and not in your head.

What is special about you usually is what comes to you naturally, even if you have the tendency to dismiss what is easy for you, because if it is easy, everybody can do it.

The first thing I do with my clients is help them connect with who they really are. I help them get a glimpse of their dreams and hold that vision so it becomes their new reality.

You can have the motivation of an army, but if you are not true to your Self, your business cannot be either. Subsequently, your clients will feel it and won't be attracted to you.

The first thing to do in your business is craft a message that will convey the story of your true Self.

4. How can you share your message in a meaningful way so you are true to yourself and true to your clients?

You need to allow yourself to live your story on a daily basis. Your message is your story: what happened to you, what it helped you achieve, what it helped you understand, and what it helped you become. As human beings we all go through transformation. It may be at different times, at different levels, or in a different manner, but once you understand that transformation cannot be avoided, it becomes easy to embrace it and to flow with it.

Sometimes the story has been buried in the deepest part of your heart for so long that it is challenging to let it out, because once it is in the open, you may feel vulnerable. And you will, of course, but this vulnerability is what makes you who you are. It is the core of your essence.

That story will position you as unique, as special. This is exactly what your family, your friends, and your clients want to see, hear, and feel from you.

Christine Marmoy helps coaches and business owners tap in to their brilliance and transform their passion and experience into remarkable businesses. She works on three levels, from discovering your brilliance, to daring to be bold, to finally claiming your spot. No stone is left unturned as she unleashes your creativity, your imagination, and your innovative power so you become unstoppable in attracting great clients and financial security. For more information, please visit www. CoachingAndSuccess.com/pebblesinthepond.

An Amazing Treasure

Colleen O'Grady, LPC, LMFT

WHEN MY DAUGHTER WAS FIVE YEARS OLD, she loved to create cozy places. Vivacious and very busy, she'd gather every pillow and blanket in the house and create a kingdom for all her stuffed animals and dolls. She loved playing dress up, which included dressing Katie, our schnauzer, in a pink tutu. Frequently she'd spin through the house without a care in the world, in what she called her pink "turnaround."

At night we would read together, say our prayers, and she'd fall asleep. Then I would spin through the house, completely preoccupied with my never-ending to-do list.

But this night was different.

It was 10:30 pm and the house was quiet. Katie was curled up on the sofa. I peeked into my daughter's room. There she was in her bed sleeping peacefully. Her face glowed in the soft light of the moon.

As I watched my daughter sleep, the minutia of the day dissipated, and my heart opened. Something woke up inside of me. I could see my daughter for her true essence – an amazing treasure. Too often the mundane things of daily routine had dimmed my ability to see this precious miracle who was my daily companion.

I needed this reminder. I didn't want to get buried in my hectic schedule and miss this amazing treasure. I made a decision to be present to my daughter and cherish her growing up years. I believed in her and wanted to be her biggest cheerleader.

Her childhood continued on in the usual way.

We took trips to the beach, pool, and zoo. We met every princess at Disney World. We played countless games of Candyland and Monopoly. We amused ourselves with pretend everything, from princess to puppy doctor. Then there were the birthday happenings, from the princess tea party to the pretend sleepover birthday party. Of course there were times when I got caught up in all the busyness, but overall my daughter was my favorite companion and she came with me on every errand.

And then she turned twelve.

(Insert dramatic music.)

Everything changed.

She'd snap at me for no reason. Suddenly she was too tall for her age, and was uncomfortable in her body. She'd run out of the room saying, "Why can't I look like all the other girls?" She looked like an eighteen-year-old, but she was very much twelve. This rocked her confidence at school. My daughter compared herself to her best friend who made straight A's, but my daughter's grades kept slipping, and so did her motivation. She had an unfortunate experience with a very shaming dance teacher that resulted in her quitting dance. My bright, creative, imaginative daughter began to shut down.

And my favorite companion turned into my biggest adversary. She didn't want to go on errands with me. Now our conversations sounded something like this:

Me: *How was school?* Her: *Fine.*

Me: *How was your history test?* Her: *NONE OF YOUR BUSINESS.*

Me: *DON'T TALK TO ME THAT WAY!* Her: *SHUT UP!*

Me: ***IF YOU DON'T LOWER YOUR VOICE AND CHANGE YOUR ATTITUDE YOU ARE GROUNDED FOR THE WEEK-END!!*** Her: *FINE. I DON'T CARE! YOU ARE A LOSER.* ***I HATE YOU.***

Wow! I will never forget the day my daughter said, "I hate you." I couldn't believe she'd said that to me. For the past eleven years I had invested my heart and soul in her well-being. I thought I had built a solid foundation for our relationship. A host of fears hit me.

"Did I lose my little girl? What is going to happen to her? Is she going to turn out like...? " Then I started in on me. *"Can I do this? Am I going to fail her?"*

Besides being a mother, I have been a marriage and family therapist, and life coach, for over twenty years. I spend my days helping families cope with life, especially mothers. And before that, I was a full-time youth minister for ten years. I was a rock star to thousands of teens and their moms. I prided myself for knowing how to connect to them.

But none of this helped when my daughter entered the teenage years.

I'd get caught up in her drama and I'd LOSE IT. Then the "therapist angel" on my shoulder would say, *"What are you doing? You know better than this,"* but I was hooked, and I'd knock the little angel off my shoulder.

Shortly after the day of "I hate you," I decided to go for a run.

About a mile into it, I thought back to the night my heart opened up and I'd watched my little one sleep. It hit me: underneath all of my daughter's drama was still an amazing treasure. I wanted to believe in her again, but I knew I needed help.

It started to turn around.

How did that happen? Well, I got a mentor. The greatest gift is to have someone believe in you. My mentor helped me rediscover my own treasure which had been buried under my worst fears. I got clear that whatever situation you may find yourself in, your best self and highest potential are always there. This was the key to turning things around.

Here is what I learned:

1. Fear doesn't serve you or your family. Don't believe your fear.

Fear creates stories that feel true, but aren't. Your imagination can spin out of control with stories that torment you and are not helpful in any way. For example, the fear "I'm losing my daughter" is a catalyst for creating stories like "She will disappear and I will never see her again," when in reality she is in the next room texting.

Believing your fear leads to losing it.

Fear drains your energy and amps up your reaction. Fear turns off the button to reason and perspective. So if you're afraid that "My daughter is going to turn out like my ex-husband," one little thing like her leaving a towel on the floor will set you off. Fear is obsessive. Eventually these obsessive thoughts will get expressed with statements like "Good luck on finding anyone who wants to marry you."

You have a choice.

You don't have to believe the fear. Check out your fear. Is it true?

If so, take effective action. If not, let it go.

2. Believe in yourself and believe in your children. Believing in your children starts with believing in yourself.

Underneath your fears is an amazing treasure – YOU. Believe in your best self and highest potential. Knowing this will quiet your fears and help you be the best mom to your children.

Belief changes everything.

I know this might sound simple, but let me share some of the changes that happened for me and my daughter by applying these principles.

I started changing, and my daughter noticed. I didn't lose it with her. I was at peace, and became my happy, playful self again. I saw my daughter differently. Once again I saw her treasure and believed in her potential. To my surprise, when I backed off and relaxed, she started changing. Her grades greatly improved. She lost a lot of weight. She pursued her passion in dance which got her into her dream high school for performing arts.

It's been nothing less than miraculous, and yes, there are still days when we both lose it, but it is rare now. Things are so different. In fact, a few days ago we were picking out birthday cards for my parents. My now fifteen-year-old daughter was being playful. She said, "Mom, if I was going to give you a birthday card, this is the one I would give you. But I am warning you Mom, it's going to make you cry." I read this beautiful poem and then my daughter said, "You're an awesome mom." She was right. I did cry.

3. When you change, the world around you changes.

When I changed, my daughter changed.

So if you want to change the world, start with yourself. What you believe matters, especially to those closest to you, because it manifests in every word you speak and action you take, even in the privacy of your own home. Even the smallest of interactions behind closed doors impacts the world. Once this energy is released from your home, it ripples into the neighborhood, schools, community, and into the world.

You change the planet every time you believe the best about yourself and those closest to you.

4. Don't try to do this alone.

Stressed-out moms often turn to other stressed-out moms for help, and what they end up doing is complaining. What turned things around for me was to have an objective person who could see me for my best self and highest potential. I now, in turn, help hundreds of other moms with their teenage daughters. There is a growing community of moms who have moved beyond their fears and see the amazing treasure in their teenage daughters.

Colleen O'Grady, a Licensed Psychotherapist and Life Coach, has had a thriving private practice for over twenty years. The mother of a happy teenage daughter, she empowers women to reconnect with their teenage daughters and reclaim their lives. Her "Power Your Parenting" program has served moms all over the country, teaching them seven steps to get back in touch with their own voice and their own power, and reconnect with their daughters. Go to www.PowerYourParenting.com to get her free ebook.

The Empowered Patient

Deirdre Dorrington, CHC, AADP

I AM MY MOTHER'S DAUGHTER and learned from her at the tender age of sixteen how to navigate through a serious illness without knowing that I was learning the vital mindset and awareness that would enable me to powerfully move through a similar experience many years later.

Cancer, which visited both of us, initially evoked fear, terror, denial, anger, disbelief, and sometimes hopelessness. Many people feel like the victim — we never did.

My mother, Edie, had ovarian cancer at a time in the 1960s when survivors were few and support groups were nonexistent. She had the traditional surgery, radiation, and chemotherapy, and shrank to 76 pounds stretched over a 5' 6" frame. The smaller she became, the more feisty, funny, and determined she was to find a way to heal.

Little did she realize at the time that she would be healing more than her physical body.

At the age of three, my mother lost her mother to breast cancer, and subsequently was placed in a convent, as her father was not able to take care of her. She was always quite innocently questioning the nuns, asking them at age seven, "If God knows everything we do, why do I need to go to confession? Why do we need to be silent at every meal? Kids need to talk." Punishment was the disciplinary action of the day for such impertinence, and she was made to sit in a dark, windowless closet. Isolation and darkness were her playmates quite a bit of the time as she continued the questioning!

At the age of twelve, she ran away from the convent. Her father and new stepmother picked her up outside the gates, took her home with them, and she achieved her goal of being in a traditional family life. To feel love again was heaven! To feel "normal" – amazing. She immersed herself in traditional school, and became the class clown and the epitome of the character actor in high school drama performances.

She met my father while working at the box office of a movie theatre where she got to see the movies for free and could learn all the dance moves. This was a good balance of expression for her, as her home life was quite stifling. She married him at the age of nineteen, and her new life began – a bit of glamour and glitz, tea dancing, and meeting lots of people who wanted to know her. She was even offered a screen test as she had the "triple threat" talent – she could sing, dance, and act, with the looks to go with them – and possessing beauty and brains made her the consummate performer (developed in her imagination required to endure the "Dark Closet"), but my father was not ready to share her with the world.

They tried for twelve years to have a family, but that was not meant to be. Adoption was their next option, and my younger brother Brad and I were lucky enough to be the chosen ones for their family. Our birthparents may have physically given birth to us, but I believe that our mom and dad were meant to be our soul parents – the ones (mostly my mother as they divorced when we were still in grade school) who were meant to raise us. She did a magnificent job giving us the gifts of her spirit that were not present in her childhood. She shared with us unconditional love, compassion, laughter, learning, and perhaps best of all, to always have an open heart and mind and to be a seeker of truth, grace, and courage, especially in trying times.

We were always aware that there was a power greater than ourselves guiding our lives, and that all things happen for a reason. You may not know the reason right now, but eventually it will unfold. Patience was another gift we received from her, because as children we wanted to know the reason NOW!

I had a happy upbringing in spite of a number of challenges and changes. My mom was always there supporting and inspiring us to do and be anything we wanted in life. Imagine how we felt the day when cancer first came to visit...

The prognosis was ovarian cancer, stage four. Back then, the options for treatment were limited and larger doses of medicines were given, which produced severe side effects. We almost lost her many times, and she had friends coming for a "Last Visit" quite often. I noticed the effects that visitors with negative energies had on Mom, and also noticed the power that optimistic people, stories, and movies had on her ability to heal. She rallied back many times from the brink of death, saying that she hadn't finished raising us, and made a promise that she needed to do that before leaving this earth. She also drew strength through the gifts from Spirit of courage, power, and grace, combined with lots of laughter. We served her healthy whole foods in small portions, creating colorful and beautiful arrays to tease her palate into eating this goodness, and made sure that she had a circle of positive people surrounding her as much as possible.

She survived for twenty years, and married a wonderful man who gave her the peace and inner security that she had missed in her child-hood. I was blessed to have both of them in my life and grateful for the extra twenty years with Mom. She lived to see her children grown, married, and starting families. She got her wish made that day in the hospital room.

To my surprise, in 2005 I was diagnosed with breast cancer. This "visitor" was not welcome in my world. As an adopted child with no genetics in common with my mother, I never thought or worried about the possibility that cancer would strike me. What was going on?

I proceeded with more testing, traditional and complementary medicine protocols, and began to interview doctors who would help me on my journey back to health. Intuitively I knew I needed to seek out all available options and then decide on the ones that would help my body heal as well as regain strength. I kept hear-ing these words in my head: "PRESERVE THE VITAL FORCE." I spent time turning inward, reflecting, journaling, and wondering if I could go through this in a less toxic way than my mom had years before.

I thought of Albert Einstein's quote: "Everything is energy." I knew that cancer is dark and dense, and the energy of healing is the opposite. There is a lightness to it when one is feeling healthy. Even without the cancer, I had been feeling a heaviness of spirit for quite some time – a heaviness deep within. Life was getting harder and more complex. I was out of balance and moving so fast that I was completely unaware of it.

My daughter was sixteen when I was first diagnosed with cancer – the same age I was when my mom was diagnosed. Coincidence? I don't believe so. My marriage was very tense and strained at that time. Was a shift in order? Would it help to remove the darker energies from my everyday life? I suddenly remembered the tension that was present in my childhood home before my mom and dad separated, and that somehow a similar pattern of behavior had been created in my own. I looked around at all areas of my life to see what I might learn, what I needed to cultivate, and what I needed to weed out.

I decided to go on a medically supervised fast to clear out any toxins that might prevent optimal healing and felt quite powerful, strong, as well as lighter, after going through the process. I then noticed that immense energy was released by the quality and lightness of the food I was choosing to eat. My new motto became "Eating for Energy," as I knew that good energy is needed to heal the body. The incentive was great to change my former way of eating, as I was going for a full cure.

My mother's tools of the spirit had helped her heal for twenty years, so I expanded on that, deciding to live to be 100, in good health, and with a vibrant spirit. When fear would come up, I would transform it immediately into optimism and hope. I am able to do this naturally, as I have fully absorbed my mother's gifts to me – the important ones that can guide you through anything with grace and ease if you can look at it in the right way.

I did need some surgery and chemotherapy, but the side effects of both were minimal. My mindset contributed to this, I am sure. I had no fear, complete trust in the Divine, and was very centered and calm inside. Less stress to the body equals more energy to heal.

I believe that any disease is in part dis-ease with some part of your life – that there is a shift that needs to happen to get back on track. This approach, along with traditional protocols and healing practices, is a truly integrative move to wellness. I took responsibility for my whole being – body, mind, and spirit – and made the changes that needed to be made in my life.

My doctor now says I'm cured — that checkups are just social visits. Maybe I can pay it forward and facilitate others' healings through my experience with cancer. I may have found the reason for the "visit"! I have no fear that it will ever return.

Deirdre Dorrington, CHC, AADP, is a Health and Wellness coach who guides people to creating a balanced diet and life through making sound nutritional and lifestyle choices. Combined with powerful stress and energy releasing protocols, she facilitates the process of transitioning from illness to wellness and struggle to ease. She is a breast cancer survivor and thriver who has navigated the journey through successfully melding traditional medicine and complementary modalities. For a guided healing meditation MP3, go to www.UniqueWellness.com.

Full Circle

Denise Wade, PhD, LMRC

"OH JESUS, PLEASE HELP ME!" I pleaded for mercy. I lay on the cold unforgiving floor, stunned and confused in the dark kitchen. His cold, hollow eyes pierced mine. His steel-toed work boot shot another bolt of pain into my skull. I fumbled for the counter, staggered, and hoisted myself up. Dizziness and nausea overcame me. A thick blanket of darkness prevented me from knowing what he would do next. Thunderous footsteps rushed up behind me. My heart raced, my breath heavy, my stomach knotted. I feared for my life.

Like an animal he hunted me in the darkness. Out of nowhere his massive forearms heaved me over his head and bent my body backwards.

"So help me God, I will break your back if you don't behave," he threatened through his slurred words, whiskey weighing heavy on his hot breath. With brute strength he forced my back into an arc, my spine sending excruciating pain throughout my body. Tears poured from my eyes and I repeatedly begged for my life. He cackled and twisted my spine harder.

My two toddlers screamed to me from upstairs. "Mommy!"

The now unbearable sting exploded down my legs. For a second I tried to make sense of who would care for my children if I became paralyzed. Not him, not this monster. He threw me over his head with inhuman-like strength onto the fractured floor beams. I lay stunned, not knowing my name, the breath knocked out of me, my feeble limbs trembling, unable to walk. I tried desperately to call to my three-year-old daughter, but my dislocated jaw would not cooperate.

Through the darkness a crash surrounded me. I could barely make out my great grandmother's china bowl, the only remembrance I had of her, shattered in hundreds of pieces. I dragged myself through the fractured debris to find the phone, desperate to be quiet so he would not hear my movements. I gasped for air, unable to draw a breath, and with every ounce of strength left I hoisted my body up, my spine screaming in agony. It was now apparent my hip was dislocated.

As I reached for the phone receiver, he returned with brutal strength and ripped the phone out of the wall.

"Who are you trying to call?" he demanded.

I dropped to the ground sobbing, unable to sustain my own weight, and called on the Divine for help. His broad shadow now hovered over my 95-pound frame. Tighter and tighter he wrapped the phone cord around my neck until my breathing became a labored effort. Reality slipped away, and I could no longer fight. This was the moment I realized that the man I loved, my beloved, was capable of killing me.

In the distance I could barely make out my one-year-old son hyperventilating from his crib upstairs. I pleaded for my life again. He zipped down his pants, ripped off mine, and said, "Be a good girl."

Then he raped me.

When he was done having his way with me, he threw me out of the house and locked the door. I stood in the frigid night screaming, bleeding, barefoot, and freezing. I had to get back in that house for my babies. I don't know who called them, but the police had arrived, and I was grateful.

My kids and I were taken to an anonymous domestic violence homeless shelter, but first we were blindfolded for our own protection. When I took off the mandatory blindfold for the first time... I saw the light. I clutched my three-year-old daughter. What kind of a role model was I? Who would protect and stand for my children? I couldn't even protect and stand for myself.

The statistics showed that 77 percent of women return to their abusers. I hated that life I had lived for twenty-five years, in my home of origin, and now as an adult. I refused to go back. I hated being one of these women at the shelter. At that moment I was bathed in shame, fear, loneliness, self-hatred, and hatred for friends and family who refused me help. I welcomed the stages of grief: denial, anger, pain, and loss. Loss of trust, loss of innocence, like a death, only it was the death of what should and could have been — the death of my girlhood dreams.

I looked across the room. I saw a prostitute detoxifying from crack. She grabbed at me and I pulled my kids tighter. Barefoot, pregnant women, their eyes swollen and blackened, were begging for money. I clutched our few belongings. These were once someone's precious little girls; almost certainly no one showed them love. As the kids and I took our designated musty cot, the smell of urine, dirty diapers, and sour baby bottles permeated the stale air.

I was startled by the cries and moans of the night. I refused to be one of the statistics. I wanted my children to have a better life. My eyes settled on my sleeping son, his hair soaked in sweat, his pajamas soaked in vomit from crying so hard, and a slow fire arose in me.

Instinctively I knew that in order to move forward I had to take personal responsibility. On some small level I was forced to examine my part in all of this. I only knew what had been modeled for me by previous generations. I was going to be the first in my lineage to break this unhealthy cycle and make a stand for myself. In the days that followed I realized that in order to survive, the first step was to forgive myself.

My anger fueled my determination to learn to love myself, value myself, and release all self-judgment. Most important, I exercised courage through the harsh court battles that followed, and fought for a Protection From Abuse Order. I endured the many false accusations from family and well-meaning friends who advised me to get over it and return to my partner for the sake of my kids. "You have too much baggage; no one will ever marry you." Instead I distanced myself from them and did whatever odd jobs I could: babysitting, waitressing, cutting hair, and cleaning houses. Eventually I was able to sustain an apartment, a job, a car, and a new life in a new city for myself and my children.

With every choice I made, I asked myself, "Will this decision move me closer to my goals?" If my answer was no, then I would refrain. My life consisted of paying bills, working, and being a single mom. I was surviving, not thriving, and I was lonely.

I bargained with God. If He would bless me with a kind and loving partner, I would spend my life serving others in any way I was called to do so. Several years later, when I least expected it, on a beautiful sunny Sunday, I mistakenly walked into a singles group at church... and there he was. I knew him when I saw him – my soul mate and best friend – and he passed my prerequisite. He loved my children as if they were his own. He legally adopted my two kids and eventually I gave birth to a baby girl. To date, we've been happily married for seventeen years and counting.

I'm no longer that frightened twenty-five-year-old girl, but a strong, confident woman who's learned to value herself. Those painful experiences ignited a passion in me to serve others in difficult relationships. I felt an overwhelming calling to return to school, and after many years I proudly earned a doctorate in Psychology and Gender Differences, and a master certification as a Relationship Expert.

Today I am grateful for the opportunity to facilitate teleseminars and workshops, and have a private coaching practice, with the goal of helping women dissolve fears, limitations, triggers, and the pains of past and current relationships. I teach self-love and empowerment to many women — married and single, teens and adults — by encouraging small, subtle shifts and challenging their outdated belief systems. My role is to gently guide them to take responsibility for their lives by first learning to forgive themselves for past mistakes and poor choices, and trusting something they may have ignored for years... their own intuition.

The best part is, I'm called to serve at a shelter for men in transition, and ironically, they very often have a history of abuse. By teaching them how to understand their own anger, I help them make their unconscious behavior conscious, and especially to articulate their needs without using violence.

Funny how that worked out, in that financially supporting this ministry and working with these men has helped me in my own quest to forgive.

If I had it to do all over again, I would. As this journey comes full circle, I see the gifts that came out of my own healing. I humbly offer them to help and empower women.

Denise Wade, PhD, LMRC, holds a doctorate in the Psychology of Relationships and Gender Differences. She is a licensed Relationship Coach. Denise recently completed a two-year relationship gender study with two thousand men and women. Her passion is helping women restore their difficult relationships, understand men, challenge their old beliefs, and transform painful relationships into positive relationships. She resides in Philadelphia with her family. She can be found at www.SweetHarmony.net.

Finally an IEP for Mom!

Doreen G. Fulton

IT WAS JULY 4TH, 1995, yet I remember the details as though it happened yesterday. I was at our community swimming pool with Greg, my oldest son, and one of his friends. Enjoying the sunshine and the laughter of kids playing in the pool, I reflected on the good life I led. I had a lovely home, a loving husband, a wonderful son, great friends, and a good job. Feeling blessed, I knew my life would soon be getting even better. Shortly, I would be getting the call... and our family would be complete.

The call came later that day and I learned that a little girl had been found for us. Her name was Sandra. She was healthy and five years old. My excitement built as I learned we had moved to first on the adoption list and I could fly to Latvia in August to meet her. As I prepared to hang up, I heard, "Sandra has a younger brother. His name is Robert. He is three years old and it would be great if we could keep them together." My mouth dropped in disbelief. At that moment, I experienced one of the biggest joys of my life.

Two months later, I brought my two younger children home from Latvia. I had spent a month getting to know them, learning about the life they had lived in the orphanage, and finalizing their adoptions in the Latvian court system.

John, my husband, and Greg quickly bonded with Sandra and Robert, and I felt immense joy and gratitude. Our family, our friends, and our neighbors joined us in celebration. Within weeks, their closets and drawers were bulging with clothes and toys. Looking back, I remember those days as some of the best of my life.

Flash Forward!

The year is now 2002, the month November, and we have been struggling with academic challenges for years now. Robert is eleven, reading at the first grade level, and our best efforts to help him have led us to frustration and anger. When his fourth grade teacher tells us he is actually regressing, we begin searching for a medical explanation. After much testing, we learn that Robert has Klinefelter's syndrome, also known as 47 XXY. He has an extra X chromosome, and like many on the autism spectrum, he has communication and social difficulties that can be helped with specialized treatment.

When it becomes clear that Robert needs more than what is being offered, we withdraw him from public school and enroll him in a multitude of special programs designed to help him with his language-based challenges. Going from one private school to another, we hope beyond hope to give him what he needs. Despite our efforts, time after time we are asked to find another school. Teachers in several schools simply do not have the skills or resources required to help Robert. We attend countless Individualized Educational Plan (IEP) meetings and still Robert struggles daily. We are gradually becoming desperate!

We enlist the help of a geneticist; see a neurologist, two endocrinologists, a psychiatrist, and a social worker; get special tutoring in reading; and still our lives continue to spiral downward. We work with Robert's psychiatrist, who experiments with a variety of medications, attempting to regulate his moods and his attention span while also working with the endocrinologist who begins a testosterone regimen.

When he is in the seventh grade we have Robert tested again, and he has not made the progress in reading that we had hoped for. He is only at the third grade level despite the intensity of instruction. Although this is disappointing news, we are thankful that Robert is enjoying his new environment, and hope that once he settles down, his academic progress will improve.

Robert starts his eighth grade year in a school that has integrated services, and just when we think he has stabilized, we get a phone call. Robert is having a difficult time socially at school; he had to be forcibly restrained by three of the staff because he was violently banging his head against the wall. The police were called and took him to the hospital emergency room. Robert spends that night in a psychiatric hospital. My heart breaks and I see my dreams begin to crumble. We worry, speak with doctors we do not know, and pray and pray for Robert's recovery.

When he is released a week later, we return to school and hope to put this incident behind us. In a closed-door meeting, we learn that Robert cannot return as a student. John and I both cry. I wonder how in the world we will survive. I wonder how Robert will react to this rejection. Where can we go? The director is very kind and is convinced that there are schools out there that can better serve Robert. We pull ourselves together, put smiles on our faces, and take Robert home.

Months Later...

I begin connecting with other parents, professionals, and school staff members who are sympathetic, and tell them that while I am happy that Robert is assimilating in his new school, I feel he needs more integrated services through which his medical, social, and academic needs can be coordinated. I even write to Oprah asking for funding. I am convinced that I will have to build a school tailored to teaching Robert. Before I can pursue this dream in full, Robert is again in serious trouble.

One night he takes our dog out for an evening walk, and without known provocation, begins shattering windows and lights at the nearby elementary school. He also breaks the windows and lights of a car on the street. He finds a vacant home and continues to shatter windows. When he gets home, he tells my husband that he heard a "voice" telling him to do so. Truly, my days and nights are beginning to be filled with fright, anger, stress, and confusion.

Another School Bites the Dust!

With growing concerns, Robert is given an opportunity to attend yet another school. The county school system is paying for the entire cost, including transportation back and forth each day. The school is run by a wonderful man, the staff is supportive, the reading teacher has developed a warm rapport with Robert, and they have special gardens tended by the students that feed the hungry in the community. Each Friday, the entire school focuses on community service, and Robert loves it!

We believe that this is an ideal situation, until one day Robert decides to run off campus. It is hot, nearly 100 degrees. He is not familiar with his surroundings and nobody knows where he is. To make matters worse, before leaving he throws a picture hanging in the hallway to the ground and the police are looking for him. I am called once again and I pray. Thankfully Robert is found, but this time he is taken to jail. When we arrive, he is released, but we are forced to secure legal counsel, go to court, and appeal to the judge.

We work with the school staff, gain their support, educate the attorney on 47 XXY, and he is then able to convince the judge to drop the criminal charges against Robert. Nonetheless, we are forced to find yet another school for Robert.

Finally, an Oasis

It is 2008, and Robert is now at a private school about thirty minutes from our home. A few days after his arrival, John and I are invited to a meeting at the school along with Robert's private therapist. Approximately twelve staff members are present. We meet the director, the counselor, the sub school principal, his teachers, and the vocational and behavioral staff. All have personally read Robert's file and are standing ready to support him.

Here and Now

Today, Robert is twenty. He is surrounded by caring teachers and guides. He has an internship, plans to graduate in June, and is gaining more independence each day. He got his driver's license on his nineteenth birthday, and while the road ahead looks bright, the terrain is unknown.

As the mom of a young adult with special needs, I know that the job market is bleak for many, yet my job as a mom continues with no end in sight. While teachers come and go, I am needed more than ever to assist my son in transitioning from school to work. To keep going, I need stamina, strength, and support, so I enjoy spending time with friends at the Oasis.

Looking back, I realize that our lives have been tremendously enriched by a caring community. We have experienced joy, success, pain, and frustration, and grown more resilient as a family. We appreciate and celebrate all strengths, and everyone is happier as a result. I have learned that transitions are seldom easy, but when we can face our challenges with those we love and admire, we often find greater meaning and joy in our lives.

With the help of my faith, my family, my friends, and my mentors, I developed my own Individualized Empowerment Plan (IEP), and "Finally, an IEP for Mom" emerged from this experience! I continue to believe in a ray of hope, and I have created an oasis of support for all. I am called to share with you the wisdom of these wonderful mentors, guides, and connectors who have made a difference in our lives.

If you know all about individualized educational plans and still struggle to find answers, please visit my website to get your own individualized empowerment plan. Finally, an IEP for YOU!

Doreen G. Fulton coaches moms of young adults with special needs and is passionate about empowering you and your child. The young adult with special challenges needs your help more than ever to support their transition from school to work. At this critical time, you may be at the end of your rope and need help to cope. Doreen offers a proven program and an online community to support you at www. IEPforMom.com. Call Doreen at (703) 371-5682.

The Best Time To Get in My Way

Dorit Sasson

"Sometimes your only available transportation is a leap of faith."
— Margaret Shepherd

I'D LIKE TO THINK THAT TEACHING English to Israeli schoolchildren was the ultimate cultural journey, but my life coach saw it as one that would allow me to connect all the dots of my life purpose and help guide me forward.

It all began in March of 2011, when she asked in an email: "Where do you think your life story could lead you – if you allowed it to lead the way? What do you think you could gain, both personally and professionally, if you came out fully with your life story?"

After years of living on a kibbutz and teaching English to Israeli schoolchildren, both my husband and I felt we needed a professional change. We decided to try our luck in a Jewish community in Pittsburgh. Unlike other newcomers from Israel we met, we didn't have friends, family, or a job waiting.

Even though I was a returning American who spoke fluent English, I felt everyone around me was speaking another language. I had left the US in 1988 as a teenager, and came back a mom and a wife almost twenty years later. "What's an SUV?" I would ask. "What's Target?" But what I was really looking for was a deeper connection to family and friends. Coming back to live permanently in the US after all those years in Israel had triggered deep and painful memories from my childhood home in New York City – mainly of social and emotional isolation.

In Pittsburgh, I didn't have the support system that most women my age with young children had, and I had another problem – I felt like an outsider. I was uprooted. At times it seemed that the strangers sitting next to me on a bus were my only family. Perhaps they could even understand me at that moment. Maybe because they looked lonely too. I didn't know how to react to this new environment at first, so I started a journal to help me cope with the social and emotional isolation I felt from sacrificing my own home, family, and friends. I recorded what people said and how they looked – no matter how painful the scenario – in order to get perspective. Sometimes the small-town mentality of Pittsburgh was too friendly and it unnerved me. Other times it was too unsettling. The theme of "finding a connection in a world of darkness" very quickly emerged in my writing.

Flashbacks were everywhere. If I heard a chopper, I would immediately flash back to the news of a terrorist attack. When I stood in front of twenty quiet, motivated, and eager ESL (English as a Second Language) adult learners, I kept waiting for that Israeli high school student to speak with chutzpah, as they say, with audacity.

During that first year, I said to my adult ESL students, "We share a global language. *I know* what it's like to live in a foreign country and be misunderstood, alone, and isolated. I know what it's like to give up everything for the sake of something new and unfamiliar." They smiled. Like a bowl of hot chicken soup, my words warmed them.

Up to that point, no one had ever "heard" or "seen" me in my writing, but in the program I had the chance to finally strip myself down. I shared some of my snippets of writing with other professional women. They loved the imagery and the feelings they evoked, and how I tapped in to my "now guidance" to help me step into my own light.

One day, I got this email from my life coach: "My very strong sense is – there's a whole new path waiting for you. It will make use of your talents as a storyteller, your training as a teacher, your very natural gifts for connecting with those who feel like they 'don't fit in,' and your brilliant gifts as a writer."

This really spoke to me. Could this be the big break I was looking for?

Being heard and seen gave me a reason to let my soul shine for myself and for others. There was a certain magic that happened in the following months, when I felt recognized and valuable.

How many times had I wanted to say something and didn't? How many times had I tried to transform the silence into something creative? When I was surrounded by other English teachers in Israel, I felt like a foreigner because everyone came from different worlds. When I was among native Israeli-born teachers, I stayed silent because I knew I was "the English-speaking American" who wasn't taken seriously.

The time had come, though, to think in terms of "business." I wanted to light the way for others and help them find a deeper connection through writing their own "pain stories."

Something, though, held back my heart. I wanted to create drama. I thought, "The teachers on my mailing list won't buy into this. School districts are too busy." I let my worries take over. I let my limiting beliefs about myself constrict, contain, and suppress me.

Beneath the pain and silence of my own story, I felt my own healing voice wanting love, desire, recognition, and compassion. All these years, I had felt comfortable "playing small" and "shrinking" so I wouldn't cause people to feel insecure. Now there was a calling for me to speak to those who were feeling some kind of disconnect.

As I started to write the book *Giving Voice to Voiceless*, I looked for models I could use to put my vision into action. I found curriculum templates online. But what I really needed to do was stop getting in my way as I had done for years. So I created a blog called "The Voice of My Life Story" that allowed me to experiment and let people see my "pain stories." For example, in the post "Finding My Tribe: From Israel to Pittsburgh," I describe the process of hearing two different voices from two different linguistic settings, always trying to remember where I came from.

I got comments like:

- "I like what you shared about acculturation."
- "Very personal and heartfelt. You have found yourself and you know where you are going. Good for you."
- "This is eye opening and should make every reader who is native to the United States have some empathy for those who have chosen to come here. Thanks for sharing your insight."
- "Wow, love this post, all the tribes we have joined, and continue to join daily!"

People were actually reading and commenting on my writing. Wow! In creation mode, my enthusiasm about my new direction jumped. The new blog made it real.

Our voices emerge when we are most honest with the painful elements of our life stories. We just need to really tune in and listen to the darkest parts of our being. I wanted, however, affirmation that I wouldn't be leaving the "teacher's shoes" entirely. I searched my inbox for more clarity from my life coach who wrote: "…you can always 'teach to teachers.' You can always 'speak on the curriculum' you've created. You can always write a book, a workbook, a manual, on the curriculum you design. You can become an expert in a particular curriculum that YOU create."

That I create. That I create. Whoa. "That's big," I thought. "That's huge."

All my life, I had tried hard to listen to be that vibration.

After signing up for a twenty-one-day Chopra Center summer meditation challenge, I finally began letting some emotional baggage go. I focused on getting clear on "Who am I? What do I want? How can I serve?" I began to live more in the here and now instead of dwelling on the past or the future. I started to let go of outcomes and put my attention on words, thoughts, and deeds in the present moment.

Know that you have the ability in every moment to break through those barriers that hinder your success and create the building blocks of your life. You have the power to transcend every limiting belief you have about yourself and do what you do brilliantly.

Releasing old emotions allowed me to be more still. In stillness and silence, my awareness of infinite possibilities deepened.

By the end of the challenge, I received my "vibrations":

Teaching and writing needed to be swirled like an ice-cream flavor.
Let the feeling part of yourself step forward. Be with the darkness.

Just a few weeks before finalizing this story, I bumped into a friend who had opened a seminary for Jewish high school graduates pursuing the arts alongside their Jewish education. She wanted to know of my latest writing project. When she heard I was writing a book, *Giving*

Voice to Voiceless, she asked with excitement, "Why don't you come and teach your curriculum to the students?"

I take this as a sign that my purpose is slowly aligning with the Universe.

And so each morning, I gracefully welcome in my tribe and all possibilities of who I can be.

Dorit Sasson is the author of *Giving Voice to Voiceless: A Five Step program to Transforming Your Life and Business in Story,* and a speaker. She uses the power of story to help others create their life and business in story. Download your free MP3, *Story Manifesto: A Guide To Stepping into the Authentic Voice and Vision of Your Story,* at www.GivingAVoicetotheVoicelessBook.com. When you do, you'll receive a complimentary subscription to the "Giving Voice to Voiceless" ezine, including a transformational tip of the week.

Who Is The Authority?

Ellen Simon, MD

IT ALL STARTED WHEN I LOST A YOUNG patient, Patricia, who unexpectedly fell unconscious to the floor. Later, in the hospital, an army of high-tech equipped medical personnel found neither a traditional cause nor a cure for her condition. Neither had I. Shortly thereafter she passed silently to the other side. I had known this young girl so well, with all her heart's pain, rejection, and loneliness. No doubt she had unconsciously chosen this as a way out of her misery.

After her death, my life was never the same, and many questions arose in my mind. Questions like "What is the function of a physician and that of modern medicine? Are we only interested in dysfunctional organs? Are patients considered no more than physical bodies? Could I have saved Patricia's life? And if so, how?" I started to question the purpose of my medical career and also my function as a mother and wife. The impact of Patricia's death was magnified by the fact that I'd recently lost the elder of my two sons as a consequence of his drug abuse.

Outwardly I seemed on top of my game. While I had both financial success and social recognition, I still felt unfulfilled. I was dying a private, inward death, and the only way I knew how to handle my unbearable pain was to shut down the connection to my heart.

I had come from a narrow, restricting, and disempowering Christian background. In traditional medicine I also experienced dogma and powerlessness. My situation felt so limiting and suffocating. I had to break out of it.

As "grace" would have it, several synchronicities pulled me in a new direction towards my hidden dreams – namely California and Buddhism. California was for me a symbol of beauty, outer freedom, and being far from everyday life, and Buddhism had a strong philosophical and religious pull on me.

I remember vividly my flight to San Francisco. Leaving my almost grown son, my husband, my office as a family doctor, and my home country made me feel numb and paralyzed. All I felt was a huge boulder of guilt, shame, and doubt weighing on my heart. Not one person had understood or approved my decision to live in a Buddhist monastery in California. Underneath the big boulder, however, grew a tiny, sparkling light of joy, strength, and certainty – something I later came to know as my "inner authority."

While California was sunny, beautiful, vast, and wonderful, the monastery proved to be far different than expected.

My daily schedule started at 5:00 am and ended between 8:00 and 10:00 pm. Twelve to fifteen hours of that time were dedicated to working. It was a completely different world for me. The work was intentionally physically demanding to counteract the conditioned Western mental orientation. There was no time for formal meditation because there was too much work to do. Work was the main practice tool. It does not cheat. Rather it shows who you are – fast, slow, organized, confused, committed, interested, responsible, careless, caring, honest, cheating, enduring, or easily giving up. Whatever your qualities or motivations are, work reveals them all. The relentless work was supposed to quiet the ongoing mind chatter and help loosen the ego games of the students – and it did! But not in a striking or rapid way.

In the monastery I did not find the peace I had anticipated, but soon I knew it would never come from my environment. It had to come from inside of me, which I had a feeling would be a long and slow process.

Many years went by. I held on to my goals of attaining inner peace and genuine happiness, finding my purpose, and realizing my full potential and the true nature of reality. I still had a long journey ahead of me to achieve these big soul goals, especially when the actual training was very grounded and down to earth, with work as the path to get there.

In my eighteenth monastic year, my health started to deteriorate. Treating myself using drugs, as I had learned in medical school, didn't help, so I went to other doctors and was prescribed more drugs. I ended up having a knee operation and a hip replacement. These medical repair shops didn't leave me feeling better; in fact, quite the opposite. Traditional medicine was not my place anymore.

Diseases don't happen out of the blue and for no good reason. Something was up. Something was nudging me. But what, and why? The answers were already on their way.

Eventually my intuition led me to an "Emotional Freedom Technique" (EFT) master practitioner. EFT is a form of Energy Psychology. At the time I didn't know what EFT was, nor did I foresee that it would open doors to the most fulfilling epoch in my life – a time that would also hold answers for my many spiritual queries.

The first healing session was surprising. The emphasis was not on what I considered my significant physical symptoms, but on my psychological and emotional history. During the EFT process, buried emotions started to emerge, and to my astonishment they gradually subsided, eventually disappeared entirely, and never returned. For my whole life, I had thoroughly suppressed it all without even noticing. In this regard the hard work at the monastery had not taught me much. The EFT work left me feeling lighter in every sense of the word – happier, more alive, and more peaceful. Amazing! This was holistic healing on all levels: physical, emotional, mental, spiritual, and energetic.

Had these few sessions been necessary to bring my eighteen monastic years to fruition? Was there actually a connection? Were these deep changes equivalent to the monastic training or were they complementary? I still don't know the answers, and I'm at peace knowing that it's likely I never will.

Instead of Buddhist literature, now I read indiscriminately about Energy Healing. My life was split between the commitment I had to the monastery and my new passion for Energy Healing. But to fully understand the depth and power of Energy Healing, I felt I needed more than just reading books. So after another full year of being only half-hearted in the monastery, I knew it was time to make the difficult decision to leave. Soon I would turn seventy-one years old.

At first I felt lonely and lost, but thankfully I found a beautiful, quiet house in California, close to the ocean, as it was an old dream of mine to live by the water. Although things seemed to be falling perfectly into place like a sanction for my decision, doubt and guilt once again ate at my heart, because my Buddhist teacher did not endorse my plans or my leaving. He seemed to consider me an arrogant and faithless student, yet I KNEW I had made the right decision. I had finally discovered that I AM the authority for my own life.

The Energy Healing I had experienced became a pivotal point in my life. My newly gained outer freedom and independence allowed me to pursue my studies in Energy Healing and Quantum Physics, to which I dedicate most of my time. Now I appreciate and enjoy every single minute of my life. A new state of being has begun for me, and it keeps expanding through my work and learning.

Energy Healing cannot be fully understood without Quantum Physics, which is awesome and mindboggling. It introduces a higher dimension and sheds a completely new light on the world – the physical and spiritual one – and actually dissolves the separating line between the two.

The deeper I study Energy Healing and Quantum Physics, the clearer it becomes to me what incredible, powerful beings we are. We are truly creators and co-creators of our lives and our realities. I envision humankind will soon embrace all the new paradigms and evolve into a species that is ready to shift with ease and grace into the "Golden World Age" – an age that is upon us now. We will all live with a higher consciousness, from the heart instead of from the mind, and from a perspective of "oneness" rather than of separation.

Different paths can manifest this evolution. In fact, when I first began to explore Energy Healing, I felt confused by all of the different modalities available. Many don't require a special gift or talent. It's even often said that we are all born healers.

Yet in other modalities, the healer sends energy from their heart to the client. My favorite modality is using Divine energy to heal, which is not something I learned from a book; rather I received this ability through a transmission from an advanced healer.

Using Divine energy is a sacred process; it changed my life more profoundly than anything ever has. Imagine directing Divine energy! Me?! I gradually began to comprehend the concept of oneness, in which we all, including the Divine, are deeply interconnected. Now Divine healing feels like a natural process, and it is truly evolutionary, because each healing or merging with the Divine raises the frequencies of the healer and of the receiver, a necessary adaptation for the new world age.

I no longer feel like I've deserted my path, anyone, or anything. Finally I know with absolute certainty that I'm pursuing my purpose. There is no going back. I am following the call to act on my insights and guidance, no matter how small or seemingly absurd. I now trust my inner authority absolutely. I'm in my power now. And the gifts I receive in return are confidence, joy, and happiness, often beyond measure. This is my wish for you, my readers, too.

After graduation from medical school in Germany, Dr. Ellen Simon and her husband opened an office in a German village. Following twenty-two years practicing family medicine, she moved to California and lived for twenty years in a Buddhist monastery. A personal health crisis in 2006-2007 sparked her interest in Energy Healing. Now Ellen lives by the Pacific Ocean studying and practicing Energy Healing.

My Mom I Wish To Call My Own

Gemma Aguilar, BA, BSc, MA

I GREW UP WITHOUT A FATHER — I was told he had died just before I was born — but with my mother, whom I couldn't call "Mom." You see, I grew up calling my mom Tita, which means "aunt" in my native tongue. She seldom took me anywhere, unlike my older sister, and when she did, she introduced me as her niece. And she made me call her Tita in front of others.

My mom was the breadwinner in her family of twelve, many of whom stayed with us before going their own way. Everyone in the family knew Tita was my biological mother, yet they played pranks on me saying that she adopted me from a sibling, which explained why I was her niece. I remember when an uncle told me that Mom tried to abort me after losing my father, at a time when this procedure was not medically accessible, but in vain. If that were true, then my life started with this death-defying experience, a precursor to other near-death incidents that I've been through. Whether that story is true or not, I've always thought

I was special; I was strong enough to save myself. Deep down, I wondered if I had done it so I could save her, too.

My older sister resembled Mom, and because I looked like my dad, I thought the pain of losing him was the reason why Mom treated me differently. Mom bought everything new for my sister, including the best cuts of meat, while I got the poor-man's staple of fish and vegetables. Mom took my sister to social events and gatherings, while I had to stay at home. I didn't mind, as I spent time with books and hobbies.

I remember always being on the sideline, observing, trying to understand why I was different from everyone else. At school events and graduation ceremonies, either no one came for me, or there was suddenly an uncle or aunt who managed to pop up at the last minute. Yet Mom managed to attend my sister's graduation or whatever event she participated in.

I remember times when I was alone and hungry and I had to fend for myself, like cooking an egg with chopped tomatoes. I learned to clean the house, do chores, and water the garden – for hours, since it was huge. I had hoped to show Mom that I could do all these things so she wouldn't have to work so hard in order to hire servants.

When friends and classmates talked about what they did with their Dad or Daddy, Mom or Mommy, I kept quiet, as these were words I did not utter. I wasn't bitter about it or jealous of my friends. I was always a joyful girl who fooled everyone into thinking I had the happiest home.

One night when I was seven, Mom was due to come home after being away many days working as a model. My sister was sound asleep. It was a stormy night, but I couldn't sleep as I waited for Mom. She finally arrived, but didn't stay. I was watching through my bedroom window, trying to get her to notice me so I could wave goodbye, but she promptly got in a car that zoomed away in a flash. I sobbed so hard it was difficult to see through the glass pane. It didn't help that rain was pouring down hard at the time. I wanted to be with her, but she had to leave for work. That was the longest time I ever cried... an episode I vowed never to let happen again.

I promised myself that I would work hard so Mom would never have to work again. I resolved to let the future make up for what had been missing in my youth. What happened that night froze in my mind and motivated me to strive for a better life for us. It seemed as though Mom's work deprived me of ever spending time with her, so I treasured every second she was home, sitting beside her while she put on her make-up, waiting to assist her with rinsing out a sponge, filling containers with water, changing water, opening lids, gluing on her false eyelashes, spraying her hair, zipping up her dress, and so on.

I watched in fascination how she could transform her looks. She was beautiful without make-up, and with it, she was sensational. The few times she travelled with us were unforgettable, though short-lived, as she would leave soon after we had arrived at our vacation home. Yet I didn't focus on what might have been or how I wanted it to be. I accepted my different life situation, as there was nothing I could have done, nor could anyone, to change Mom or her circumstances. It wasn't like something I had had and lost that I should feel sorry about. Instead, I resolved not to repeat the cycle if I had children, but to change it. I knew that despite my background and situation, it was clearly my life purpose to help her transform to be more in touch with her reality as a mother, and to give my own kids the values, virtues, and faith they would need to nurture while they were still young.

In my last year of high school, I wanted to graduate with honors so that I would get accepted into the best college, and I did. I succeeded and was one of only two from our school to be privileged to attend the most competitive and prestigious private university in my country, usually reserved for males, which had recently started accepting more women entrants.

In my freshmen year, I took an exam to join the university paper, and surprised myself when I was judged highly by a jury that included prominent Philippine writers and directors, and was appointed Features Editor. A year later, I got the News Editor position, which I combined with my first bouts at freelance volunteer work at wire agencies and public tabloids. I graduated *summa cum laude* and finished two degrees in four years.

My detached relationship with Mom made me strong, independent, and fearless. Growing up distant from her made me understand who I was and rely on no one but myself. Mom made me see that there was nothing to lose and everything to gain, so each time I aspired to something, I persevered and succeeded. She made me as confident and sure as I am, as I have been, and as I ever will be. As contradictory as it might seem, I attribute my strength to her stout sense of detachment.

My mother made it easy for me to leave at a young age and go places without ever feeling guilty that I would cause her worries or pain. I learned how to survive from everything that I had been through in life. By far the most important thing she bequeathed to me was freedom to become myself and live a life of my own. So I discovered myself and explored my potential beyond imagination.

I had a short but purposeful and fulfilling writing and teaching career in the Philippines, and then got accepted to a prestigious school in Montreal, Canada, where I lived for many years, accomplishing much at work, study, and volunteer undertakings. In the process, I've grown to love my mom more for what she made me become. To this day, we still have that detached bond that's oddly very strong.

Many times in my life I've seen relationships between mothers and children that are pitiful, contemptible, pathetic, or shameful. I often wondered why the world was complicated. Why did people take many things for granted? Why can't every person accept their uniqueness and let go of the ego that judges what's good and bad? When people focus on what's wrong and missing, it only makes them victims, while if they accept themselves and things as they are, it sends out a positive charge that draws them closer to their true nature — how they were meant to be. There's an inner power that people possess and can tap in to. Some call it luck, and some call it divine intervention, or a miracle.

The last time Mom introduced me as her niece was three decades ago. Yet I still say "Tit" (short for Tita) when I call her, but it's just a title. I do tell her each time we talk on the phone that I love her and she tells me the same. As a kid, I always felt blessed to be alive at all. Now I'm forever grateful to her for my life, which has been colorful and wonderful. Each time I look back at my life, I realize that the most precious possessions I have are memories of Mom. Though my relationship with her was not a continuous, smooth flow, it included experiences that are unforgettable. Those moments possessed clarity, energy, and vitality that formed a field with a ripple effect around them, creating bigger waves of thoughts, dreams, and implications. I cherish them and count on them for the lessons learned and choices made.

Gemma Aguilar, BA/BSc/MA, did graduate/post-graduate studies in Political Science/Teaching Education, took up Broadcast Journalism/French/Dutch/Japanese, and worked as a teacher/journalist. A controversial editor at a prominent Philippine university, her stories ignited debates within/outside the academia. Writing for an Asian magazine and the sole alternative paper against Marcos's regime often triggered tension and dispute, contributing to her short-lived career. Having left the Philippines at twenty-one, she started a teaching/writing profession in Canada and the Netherlands. Discover more at www. GemStarInfoSolutions.com or www.Gemma-Aguilar.com.

I Can't Do It Anymore

Heather Greenaway and Kim Pointon

IT WAS A VERY COLD AND BRILLIANT DAY when I looked out the window to see that the walkway had yet again not been shoveled. Instantly my temper rose as I grabbed my coat and boots and went outside to clear away the snow. As I threw the first shovelful, I could feel the anger building in me. "Why is it me who is doing this? It's NOT my job! Why do I have to do everything, especially physical chores? I am a woman, not a man!" Old issues came flooding into my mind, adding fuel to the fire.

When I was halfway done, I was in a rage, and by the time I reached the end of the walkway, my shoulders gave out completely. I had to stop and lean on the shovel for support as the tears came — tears that had been held inside me for a long time. It seemed that all the old wounds kept opening up — things that had long since passed, and yet they were in my mind as if they had happened just that instant.

As I wept, a realization came over me that I had to let go of this anger. I couldn't carry it any longer, as it was eating me up. My life and my relationships were at an all-time low. I was angry with everyone

— my co-workers, my family, my husband. Nobody was doing what they were supposed to do. I felt I was the only one doing anything and no one else seemed to care. Could they not see how I was struggling? What was wrong with them? Well, one thing I knew at that moment was that I would not be shoveling again any time soon with my shoulders the way they were, so to hell with them all!

I dragged the shovel back to the door and came into the house calmer, having had my meltdown outside. Then I began berating myself for what I was feeling. I became resolved to the fact that there was no use in trying. Nothing was ever going to change. I would quietly deal with my sore shoulders and just set aside my anger. That would be the end of it.

However, this was not to be the case, as other things cropped up and the anger was always there. I again thought that I needed to resolve this anger, as it would not go away, and when I talked to those involved, it ended in chaos. Where was I going to get help? I didn't want anyone to know that I was having a problem — that wouldn't look good. So I had a conversation with God, whom I was angry with for getting me into this situation in the first place! "Where do I go? What do I do? What's wrong with me that I can't resolve this issue? Why doesn't anyone care about me?" After asking all these questions and wallowing in my pity party, I still didn't have a clear answer. However, I did feel better.

Not long after there was a posting at my workplace about a Reiki Master who offered a number of treatments. On this sheet was an emotional healing treatment. My eyes were drawn to that particular one, and even though I didn't have a clue what this energy work meant, I somehow knew that I was to do this treatment. It was strange and a little unsettling for me, as I didn't do any research about this person, her practice, or the energy work she was doing. Interestingly enough, I felt that there was no need to.

When I went for the appointment and met the practitioner, again I knew that this was right for me. She asked what it was that I wanted to heal and I said that I didn't want to be angry anymore! It was one of the most beautiful and profound treatments I have ever had. It was as if a dam had broken and all the polluted water was bursting forth, gushing out of me. This woman comforted me and gave me the space to grieve and to let go and to find room in my heart for myself and others. My heart was toxic, and when we were done it felt clear and light for the first time in many years. Even the pain in my shoulders had disappeared! I left there feeling hope that not all was lost. This was the opening that I needed – my rebirthing had begun. God had stepped into my life!

Between that day when I shoveled the walk and the day that I saw the Reiki posting was a critical point in my life, when I started to talk to God and my story was heard. At that time I was unaware that I had finally surrendered, and said, "I need help." By His/Her grace, I was guided to the person who could help me find my way. When my true healing began, I came to understand that it was not a coincidence that this practitioner showed up in my life. When I had reached out, God was there, ready, willing, and able to show me the way.

This woman was the one to nurture me while I went through this challenge and others. Before this, I sensed that I was on the path to my home and that the door was always open, but I had just lost sight of that fact. Now I started to see that there was a light at the end of the tunnel. No matter how dim, it was there. The light that I could see opened me up to alternative healings, energy, and intuitive work, and I knew that I had started to find my true path. I became a Reiki Master, and there was purpose behind that decision.

I got a call from a young woman named Heather, and little did I know at the time the impact she would make on my life. They always say that a client comes to you for a particular reason, and the question to ask is, "What is it that I need to learn today?" Together we realized that she, too, was angry, feeling unloved and unsupported, and doing it all. Being a young mother and business owner, there were never enough hours in the day to get everything done, and certainly no time for her to love herself. I knew that we were intended to come together, as we were mirrors for each other in our lives.

With this recognition, together we moved through the hurt and pain, and we found our way. We understood that there are times when we all need to ask for help and support one another. Just as God had sent me the Reiki Master, God had sent me Heather to move further along my path and to heal. I knew that love and support and all the things that I had been looking for were mine to give to this woman. Together we recognized that healing comes from the inside first, not from the outside. We didn't understand at the time that it was our choice to experience lives filled with challenges, struggles, and heartaches. When we were in the depths of it, we were both asking, "Why? Why me?" We now realized that we had, and have, choices, and we had to experience what we had experienced in order to be where we are now. This makes the gifts we received that much sweeter.

As we continually move forward in discovering our authentic selves, sometimes the process moves quickly and at others not so much, and that's okay. We work at the rate and speed that God intended us to.

My life has changed for myself and those around me, and the same has happened for Heather. We have been able to let go of control and let be what is meant to be. We have realized that love starts with each of us, and that when our cup is full, it flows everywhere. We are both forever grateful from the deepest part of our hearts to God and to those we have chosen to be with in our lives.

Even though we may feel alone in our life struggles, we never are. Reach out and find the hand that is extended to you and take hold of it. Only you can make the connection.

Kim Pointon is a Reiki Master and an Ordained Spiritual Minister of Peace. She is ever evolving along her path to becoming her authentic self. Heather Greenaway is a Registered Massage Therapist and Certified Bowen Practitioner, Reiki. Heather's passion is to help people move into wellness. Together Kim and Heather combine their gifts to help others. For more information please visit www.Health-Works.ca to receive a free distant healing treatment.

Transform Chaos into Order

Dr. Huesan B. Tran

THE EXTERNAL CHAOS OF THE GREATEST shift in human history demands clarity to restore order, and the answer is in self-awakening. When I made the decision to give up my management consulting career to be a servant of God, and moved from Hong Kong back to Los Angeles in 1998, my journey of attaining self-mastery began. I had a calling to prepare myself to serve in time of chaos, crisis, and collapse; it is uncertain when that future will arrive and how things may unfold. Before the financial and economic chaos and crisis happened in 2008, I was going through chaos in my life to finally connect the different random dots to see the big picture to find clarity, direction, and order.

Since 1997, I have known who I am, why I am here, and what I am here to do, but I did not have the "how" to do it. As I went through over a decade of struggles between the spiritual and physical realms, looking for a way to integrate both worlds, I wondered how I was ever going to fulfill my soul purpose and divine mission on Earth.

The world is like a jungle with no path. I was seeking everywhere, but was completely stuck and living in chaos and disorder. There were many resistances and trials coming from all angles – family, friends, social, career, business, finance, etc. I explored every means possible and found myself all over the map in so many different industries. Looking back, this process helped me recognize the common underlying problems in various industries and how to make corrections. The old way of separation and disintegration does not work, and the new way had yet to be invented.

I knew I had to invent the new way, and the only way to do so was to keep trying, through trials and errors, as most inventors have done. I tried and failed at many things, but never stopped and never gave up. It was a lonely and isolated experience that few understand. I looked for mentors, yet couldn't find any. So many teach with tunnel vision, focusing on a niche within a niche, which is very remote from the calling I am here to do. Many coaches forewarn that if no keyword exists on Google, then there is no audience, and I will starve. These coaches are right in a way, but not totally.

If the internet had been available in Buddha's and Jesus's times, and they had waited for Google keyword searches in order to bring forth the new teachings of God, the world would be stuck forever. It is the responsibility of the aware to wake up the unaware. Bridging the gap of consciousness is the duty and mission of messengers and change agents.

The greater the mission, the greater the hardship.

The struggle to bring new creation and new teaching to the world is a normal process. Many great masters and teachers in history made sacrifices to bring forth new vision and great work to the world. Many had gone through a similar path of losing everything to gain everything. The process of losing everything is the process of detaching from the old to be free from culture, tradition, system, and old paradigms that don't fit anymore, so that new paradigms can emerge.

The very worst that happened turned out to be a true blessing that taught me lessons no school can teach. This is the way to experience what's wrong with the world and uncover the root of the problem, which leads to the discovery of solutions and new breakthroughs. When there is no existing mentor, you are the first to walk the path and become a mentor to those who come after you on a similar path.

The work of a pioneer is beyond conventional ways. Pioneers create the path from the inside out, because there is no path to follow. I finally realized that I just have to be who I am and create my own path, because no other way will work. The irony is that even though I knew this, I still struggled.

One night, when I felt so tired, exhausted, and stuck, I had to know what was blocking me that I didn't see. I asked God why I hadn't attained the success that I was supposed to have with all the gifts, talents, education, knowledge, skills, and experience, etc. that I have.

Here's God's reply: "It is an identity issue."

That was when I woke up and realized how my internal identity and external identity were so misaligned. How could people know who I am and what I can offer to help them if my external identity is so not me? How could I be fulfilled if I am not being myself and doing what I am meant to do?

The reason for not having success or having limited success is confused energies, or misalignment of internal and external energies. Confused energies trace back to the misalignment of internal and external identity. All the strategies and tactics do not matter until your identity is clear for you and for those you are meant to serve. That is the clarity of who you are, your vision, your direction, your passion, how you help people, why they should work with you, and your value or contribution to the world.

The identity issue is a common problem for many enlightened entrepreneurs and heart-centered people who limit their blossoming into doing what they love and fulfilling their dreams. Integrating spiritual work in the business world is challenging because business, marketing and sales, and job training teach you to match what the market or employer wants rather than being who you are. So your originality and energy never come out authentically. That is why your outer voice is not congruent with your inner voice. You can make a lot of money, yet still be limited and not feel right. Until both internal and external identity is aligned into one, life and career will continue to be in chaos or struggles, or unfulfilled.

There are endless lessons I can share with you, but the most important lesson for living your true identity is self-mastery. Self-mastery is when the internal you and the external you are "One." That is knowing and living your true self, being who you really are and doing what you are here to do, so that you are aligned with your soul purpose and divine mission.

To attain self-mastery, there are three major steps. The first is to get clear on who you are and your unique gift, purpose, and mission. If you do not have clarity in regard to these, life coaching will help you get clear faster than trying to do it on your own. The second is to align your internal identity with your external identity so others can know the real you. The third step is to align your real identity and how you serve with what the market wants and will pay for.

It is your duty to communicate what you do, why you do it, how you serve, and what solutions, values, and benefits you bring to people.

Once you have clarity to align and integrate everything, your energy flows smoothly, easily, and effortlessly, and your business, career, and profession become an extension of who you are from the inside out.

The world is trapped in the outside-in approach. The right approach is to start with the core from the inside-out, then align the inside world with the outside world.

What appears chaotic, random, and separated in the outer world is actually connected with the inner world. Chaos is a higher order of creation. All the random dots eventually plot a big picture over time.

For years I was torn between the energy healing field and the financial and wealth management field. I finally realized that the answer to my struggle was not to choose one or the other, but to embrace and integrate both into one. That is how I integrated energy healing philosophy with financial and economic healing to create a new financial paradise.

The current system we live in trained us to think and function with a one-track mind – one career, one specialization, one niche, etc. The problem with niche and specialization is fragmentation and disintegration that loses sight of the whole picture. It is important to have both vertical and horizontal integration in life, business, and career, as well as inner integration with your true identity so you are aligned with your soul purpose and divine mission. Holistic integration is a must to bridge all gaps to transform chaos to clarity to order.

Success and wealth follow order, clarity, and focus, because that is where and how energy is directed. What you do is an extension of your energy. Let your true identity show, because that is how your energy and light reaches the ones who have been looking and waiting for you. True success in life is knowing and living your true self to fulfill your soul purpose and divine mission.

The world we live in is a projection of our energy and consciousness. Chaos of the external world is a reflection of the chaos of the internal world. Chaos is the mismatch of internal and external identity. Order is when the external and internal identities are aligned so you are being who you are, living your true self. When everyone is living their true identity, the world will be transformed from chaos into order.

Dr. Huesan B. Tran (HuesanTran.com), Transformational Author, Speaker, Spiritual Teacher and Visionary Leader of the New Paradise, integrates energy healing philosophy into business, finance, and economics to transform lives to the new paradigm. She invented the revolutionary NEW WEALTH MODEL™ which utilizes innovative risk-free and tax-free strategies to create wealth, higher purpose, and mission. Her seminars and expert series provide both conceptual understanding and practical solutions for healing, rebuilding, and creating a New Financial Paradise™. Join her FREE teleseminars on www.NewFinancialParadise.com.

Touching Spirit

Jacqueline Jordan, PhDc

"In our sleep, pain, which cannot forget, falls drop by drop upon the heart, until in our own despair, against our will comes wisdom through the awful grace of God."— Aeschylus

AS A YOUNG MAN, AESCHYLUS AWOKE from a dream in which the god Dionysus commanded the future playwright to write his first tragedy. Taking the dream at face value and putting pen in hand, he thus stepped into history as the Father of Greek Tragedy.

Reminiscent of similar revelations found in literature, the Bible, and the annals of humankind, such encounters become transformative by virtue of the profound lessons taken to the heart by those upon whom they are visited. Becoming wise requires some degree of sacrifice, pain, trust, even embracing the awe-full grace of God. Wisdom – a pearl of great price – thus emerges from the upending occurrence I call Touching Spirit.

I am neither a prophet nor a seer, yet like Aeschylus, certain futures have been divulged to me as Spirit saunters in, nudges me to listen up, and further cautions I'd best be sitting down. Taking no chances, I am usually prone.

My first acknowledged experience of Touching Spirit was just prior to the birth of my only child. I awoke in a cold sweat from a dream — terrorizing, real, and portentous. In spite of a near-perfect pregnancy, in my heart I knew my baby would have grave challenges in birth and in life. The underlying prescient warning from Spirit and my own trepidations were spot-on.

My Halloween baby boy was gorgeous, and I adored him! But early on there were potential problems, and grand-mal seizures became the new norm while Greg remained in the neo-natal ICU. As we anxiously awaited signs of developmental progress, we watched Greg's body thrive, but no neurological improvements were forthcoming.

The following April, he was formally diagnosed with a rare brain abnormality, the sixth such recorded case. As laypersons, even we could see on the x-ray that parts of his brain were over-developed, while empty spaces existed where there should have been grey matter — a devastating result of the embryonic cellular division process gone haywire.

The radical prognosis was the undoing of my brief mothering experience. Greg would never hold up his head, sit up on his own, roll over, crawl, walk, talk, or feed himself. He would be completely dependent on others for everything in life.

The answer to the resounding question of his life expectancy was perhaps twenty-five years, perhaps not. My precognitive dream came crashing down on me and mine as I realized there were inexplicable, unnamed forces at play in my life. I had not yet made friends with Spirit.

Life with our special-needs son was challenging, and as Greg grew in weight and physique, it became clear we would soon be in need of help caring for him. At one year, he was thirty-six pounds of dead weight, exacting a physical toll on me. Six months later, we made the painful decision to place him in a community home with five other developmentally disabled children. So began the process of getting on with life and the accompanying guilt.

Months later, Spirit touched me yet again, revealing an unmistakable message: My son would die before his seventh birthday. Never questioning its veracity, I accepted that our time together was finite, and I put every facet of him to memory: his champagne-colored hair, silky-soft skin, deep blue eyes with long black lashes, and his loopy grin of amusement. Nestling his body against mine granted me a lifetime of loving memories.

With each of Greg's birthdays, I was mindful that I was one year closer to losing him. And finally, I did. Early in the morning of September 28th, 1975, the Marin County Coroner called us with the sad news that Greg had passed peacefully during sleep. It was one month, three days before his Halloween birthday, which would have been his seventh.

Grateful for Spirit's warning, I would not trade those precious moments with my son, writing his essence on my very soul, trusting in the knowledge that our time was limited. *Thank you, Spirit, for being my trusted confidant.*

Touching Spirit occurrences are always revelatory, arriving as warnings, reminders to get one's act together or to slow down. Some contain hope and promise for the future, while others grant a view into coming events, seemingly out of our control to prevent. However, as seasoned as I was becoming with Touching Spirit, I was still humanly fallible, and kept my head in the sand.

As the owner of two retail stores in San Francisco, I was one busy gal. One day, I was stopped cold with a remarkable vision of myself trying out crutches. Briefly rubbing my eyes, I soldiered on with my busyness. Even after three or four repetitious visions that week, I did not stop to contemplate the inherent deeper meaning of Spirit's latest touch.

In the end I paid dearly for my inattention, falling down our back steps, landing ten feet out on a flagstone walkway. My shattered heel required extensive surgery followed by intensive physical therapy, and I did not return to work for one year. As for trying out crutches – a replication of my prescient psychic flashes. *Thank you, Spirit, for the reminder to be fully present.*

Four years later, Spirit touched me repetitively as I awoke morning after morning with a heavy knowing that my husband would die of cancer. Jim's father had died of bladder cancer at forty-two, so it was a strong possibility. Should I tell him? Perhaps we should take out life insurance? (In hindsight, we should have, for the cancer might have been discovered sooner.)

I awoke daily to the niggling reminder, but remained mute, stymied in indecisiveness. I knew telling Jim would devastate him, given his cynicism towards such prognostications and his fear of death. Remaining silent, I allowed my own fears to get the upper hand. Perhaps on another level, I was at one with Spirit, acquiescing to a bigger plan that was playing out on life's landscape.

Six months later, Jim was indeed diagnosed with a particularly virulent lung cancer. Despite thirteen months of therapies, chasing metastatic tumors that blew through him like a forest fire, he was gone. Spirit does Her best, but we are still free spirits ourselves, with free will to do as we choose with our lives and our loves, sometimes exacting heavy prices. Thank you, Spirit, for teaching me the hard lessons.

Years later, while facilitating bereavement groups, one night I awoke from a poignant dream of an elderly widow unable to share her grief with her family. In the dream I embraced her, stressing that her true strengths lay in sharing all of herself with those who loved her. Out of the depths came a sonorous booming voice, "This is the work you were born to do." Like Aeschylus, I heeded Spirit's touch, entering a master's program focused on Grief Therapy. My unintended academic career thus launched, I am now a dissertation away from completing a doctorate in Psychology. *Thank you, Spirit, for illuminating my path.*

In the wee hours of September 10th, 2001, while attending an academic residential retreat, I awoke from a prescient dream of a skyscraper collapsing, twenty-four hours before the actual event. Observing the clogging mass of black plumes of smoke and the ensuing chaos of desks, file cabinets, and papers collapsing down into the building's central core, I observed a terrified young man, his face frozen by fear. The dream was over in one wretched moment, but his visage is etched in memory. Like my psychic flashes of years before, the visions returned that day, time and again, leaving me helpless to intervene and inexplicably crying buckets of tears.

The following morning of 9-11, as yet unaware of the horrific events taking place back East, while showering, a firm voice informed me, "You are to write a book titled *Mother's End*."

What kind of crazy title is that?

"About mothers who have lost a child, signifying the end of that mothering experience."

Oh. Cool title. Perfect.

Our group was packed, ready to return home, but our leave-taking was interrupted by the explosive news of that memorable day. Much later, I contemplated Spirit's impeccable timing, informing me of such a future undertaking within moments of nearly three thousand mothers losing their children. Spirit's exquisite touch cannot be ignored, and the premise of *Mother's End* is germinating — ten years' worth — and will be in perfect alignment with how it came to me and came to be. Stay tuned. *Thank you, Spirit, for your guidance.*

So... what would YOU do with Spirit Touches?

Do you consider such revelations resting somewhere on the future horizon of your life a blessing or a curse? Moreover, would you trust that these messages are indeed from Spirit? How might you react... or would you?

Regardless of the questions posed, our reactions directly correlate with who we are as human beings. Perhaps more to the point, who we become in the process of becoming. For in some vital way, Spirit's touch transforms us, our worldviews, and our very lives.

But really, it is about coming to embrace the promises Spirit divulges, to trust and acknowledge that She is wise and loves us enough to empower us with future truths. Engaging ourselves in loving what we have in those fleeting moments of having, we can be then transformed by Spirit's touching nuggets of wisdom.

Are you up to the task?

Jacqueline Jordan, PhD(C), is a doctoral candidate majoring in Psychology at Saybrook University, focusing on Consciousness and Spirituality. Her research addresses forms of exceptional human experience. Additionally, she holds certificates in Socially Engaged Spirituality and Grief Therapy. When not considering the mystical, metaphysical, and spiritual aspects of life, she returns to earth as a design and marketing consultant. For her blogs and pertinent resources, she invites you to visit her website, www.Touching-Spirit.com.

Grace Reveals It!

Jane Hunter, Dip Counseling/Teaching

IT WAS 2007, AND I HAD JUST TURNED FORTY, when life revealed itself to itself in a sudden awakening. All seeking and any and all suffering came to an abrupt and final end. It was a radical waking up to the illusion of this dream, which has been, and continues to be, the most simple, the most obvious, and the greatest revelation or blessing of this life.

I guess you could say that I had been a spiritual seeker of some sort or another for most of my adult life, always looking into what could improve "me," or better my life in some way. I had a belief that all this seeking and sincere effort would end up with my finding enlightenment (or something like that) sometime in the future. It would all add up in the long run, perhaps even in a future life. I couldn't have been further from the truth.

Although I had experienced heartache and loss, I still felt my life was a happy one, but like most people, I had to admit there was still a subtle undercurrent of discontent, often accompanied by the thought "Surely, surely to God, this can't be it! There has got to be more to life than this!"

What a surprise to discover that this thought and all that outer seeking and soul searching would be the very thing that would keep me from recognizing the eternal and boundless truth of Self!

My greatest love is to enliven what is already alive and well within you, so that you, too, can experience the vast sense of well-being that is always present, and know unequivocally that well-being is the reality, and discontent is merely the illusion.

If you have heard the eternal call to come home and return to the deep, then know in your heart that it is easy, because your heart knows this: It's only your mind that thinks otherwise, and you can't trust the mind!

If you are honest with yourself, you may see that you have been living pretty much on the surface of life, which can never fulfill you in the way that living from the depths can. It's in the still, deep waters of your "Being" that you are held and nourished, and where you have an enormous facility to be with everything, a capacity you knew existed but until now you couldn't quite expand into.

There is nothing wrong with the mind — it is innocent, too. However, the mind contracts the expansion or free-feeling experience of life because the mind is limited. Yet when the mind or "ego self" is transcended, and all beliefs are blown, you will see through this deception, and then a very natural and miraculous thing will occur; you will gently and naturally relax back into life as life, and simply enjoy the ride as an ordinary human being. You will be totally liberated from the concerns of this world, but have utter love and compassion for it. This total waking up is not what you think it is; it is a complete liberation, and you can just rest, be yourself, and let everyone and everything just "be" as well.

Let me be frank. I am an ordinary human being just like you. It's simply that I now live in an innocent, free-feeling experience of life in which the "human" and the "being" have come together; in which the self and "no self" have aligned, and in which nothing can stick or have any real charge to it anymore, as it can all pass through. This return to innocence is what transforms this life in the most sublime way. It's a humble love, exquisitely intimate, and you find you are naturally in love with the everyday, the commonplace, and with everything and everybody, since it is all only you.

Many of you reading these words have been searching for enlightenment like I once did. Initially the seeking is right, but it is also the very thing that stops you from realizing you! The seeking is a fool's game, just as enlightenment is a great myth. They keep you in the search, but never finding the star of your own sweet self, the source of all life.

So here's a chance to stop, relax, and return all seeking back onto you so that you can implode back in on yourself, as prior to time and space.

You may ask, "How do I do it, and how do I get it?"

Well, you may not like hearing this, but there really is no "how." There's nothing to get, and there really is nothing you can do! However, there is one thing that life does, as you, and that is at some point it will declare that you are its own. And the day will come when it will just start to dawn on you, or it will happen unexpectedly, or both, as it did in my case.

First, let me tell you about a little bird called the kingfisher, because in the sacred traditions, it holds the mantle of vigilance. The little kingfisher stays alert, still, and keeps the silent vigil with itself. Like that of the kingfisher, the vigil with yourself is not hard or rigid; rather it is a soft and gentle attention to yourself, just as yourself, which can take you to the heart and Source of life itself, "The Absolute."

This gentle vigil allows you to be receptive and to be an open conduit for grace, because it is in this receptivity that your deliverance is revealed. All is radically redeemed and you are free just to be exactly who and as you are. It is the greatest relief and the deepest relaxation, because nothing can ever be taken too seriously after that. You will hold everything lightheartedly, yet with deep profundity, and this will birth within you an immense capacity for compassion. When you can no longer take anything seriously, not even someone's death or your own death, for that matter, then this is true transformation, because when all fear of death and the death of others disappears, you will know yourself to be the deathless and the eternal.

It is only in lightheartedness that you can reach the depths of simple sweetness in life, and in that openness you live in everyday beauty. This is the miracle of life.

You may think, "It can't be that simple! There has got to be more to it than just being still with yourself." That very statement itself shows that you are still in the seeking mode, that you are still looking for something more or something better, still trying to improve you. When the need to seek subsides or stops altogether, you are home. This may happen slowly or suddenly – it doesn't matter. Most people just can't fathom that it could be so simple, and therefore dismiss it.

But what if I were to say to you, "This is as good as it gets, folks." Right here, right now, is more than enough, because the freedom that comes with full awakening is radical acceptance. It is not the freedom from anything, but rather it is the freedom to be with everything. It's not to escape anything, but to include it all.

No matter its appearance, whether it appears as the dark or the light, the good or the bad, or the painful or the blissful, because there is a radical knowledge underneath and inherently at the core of all appearances that everything is the Self. That's why it's difficult to judge anything after that.

Surprisingly, in just one moment of pure vigilance, the struggle ceases as you turn your attention or your awareness to yourself first, not to the thoughts and feelings, and not to any type of meditation per se, but just to you just as you are. You break the circuit and hypnotic trance of all your stories. This is how struggling or resistance collapse and unwind. At some point, the mind gets blown and all concepts and beliefs you ever held, even the dearest and most sacred beliefs, get blasted, and this is what it means to be free.

In keeping the vigil, eventually you transcend the self, then the "ego self" cannot assert itself like it did before, because you can no longer believe in it. Your identity is no longer limited. When you see that you belong to the vastness of all that is, and that you are all that is, you see that this was always the case. This is part of the great transformation and this brings with it a fresh new way and ease of being in life.

When you do this one thing in the midst of everything that is going on, you will touch the "real." The "real" is nothing to speak of; it's just nothing. You keep noticing that you exist, and in that you will notice the full, alive nothingness, and the stopped, bright stillness. This is the "real!"

Now here is where it gets interesting, because it is this vigil, this receptivity, that acts like a magnet and calls forth grace, as it is only by grace that one realizes. You don't self-realize; grace reveals it. It reveals that you are fully and completely already realized, awake, and home. In fact, you see that there is nothing to realize. It is the great mystery, because you discover that there is no one there, there is "no self" to realize! And that's the big cosmic joke!

So be like the little kingfisher and keep the vigil. Then you are a magnet for grace and when you least expect it, grace takes you home

Jane Hunter is an experienced Counsellor and now acts as a Truth of Life Guide and Freelance Writer. She is a way shower in the simplicity and easy grace of Realization and the practical embodying and living of this in everyday life. Visit www.JaneHunter.org to learn more about Jane and receive a free video series called *Grace Reveals It!*

Trust the Roller Coaster of Life

Jane St Catherine, BSc

THEN
Journal Extracts:

March 2003

I'm slipping backwards past the point of no return. I feel as though I'm clinging to a branch on the bank of the river with my nose pressed up against the mud and my hands aching from holding on so tightly. My body is tense with struggle and fear. I can't move. I can barely breathe. I'm scared. God, I wish I could turn it all around.

I need to trust, just trust that it will work. I'll have to let go and ride this raging torrent my life has suddenly become. I'm stretching my boundaries, testing my limits. I've been willing to step out of my comfort zone, to have a go at something I believed in my heart would benefit me and others. I've put my house up as security to purchase an investment property with some other people, and they've stopped making their payments.

As I tried to meditate this morning under a big tree in the Botanic

Gardens, my heart was thumping and my guts were churning. I know this is all part of the bigger picture of my life and will contribute to my spiritual growth, but sometimes I feel as though I'm losing my mind. There are two things I need right now — advice, and some new programming in my brain. My courage and strength are waning.

I sold my precious motorbike for less than half its insured value, and walked home in tears to be greeted by yet another one of those disgusting envelopes from the bank. The mere sight of the envelope caused my heart to skip a beat, but didn't immediately ruin my day.

Then I opened it.

This one was different.

This one stated in **BOLD CAPITALS** that if I didn't pay thousands more dollars I didn't have, my home in Canberra, the culmination of twenty-five years of hard work, would be gone in seventy-two hours. The pain hit me in the gut. I felt as though I'd fought twenty rounds with Mohammad Ali and then fallen off my motorbike on the way home.

I can't make all those payments alone, and there's certainly no way I can pay next month's rent on this lovely, sunny apartment where I'm living in Melbourne, so I'll have to pack up and move.

But where to? I'll whittle my stuff down again. Some part of me actually feels happy to take what I can carry and go on life's roller coaster not too heavily burdened with stuff. For the last couple of weeks I've been looking under all the bridges and trying to find a safe place to live.

Sasha, a kind young colleague, took me to the supermarket to collect some empty packing boxes. I would have preferred food.

May 2003

Last night, walking home from work in despair, feeling very broke and wondering where I'll move to, I walked past a man sitting on the footpath who asked me for a dollar. I just walked straight past without acknowledging him, although I was aware of him and his request. I felt disgusting after I'd done that, telling myself that I couldn't spare a dollar. Although I've barely eaten for weeks, I had an unfortunate need to spend my last couple of dollars on chocolate. Then I went back to the man with my change and gave him my last dollar.

I squatted on the footpath beside him and searched his eyes for answers. In that moment I felt safe and not alone. What's his story? Will I be living on the street too? I shared my Kit Kat with him and wondered how he ended up there, how others end up millionaires, and whether I'll be blessed enough to know both ends.

He touched my soul. What little trigger or pattern put him on the street, and what almost puts me there but will surely save me from it at the last minute?

How can I understand the triggers, beliefs, and patterns that shape our destiny? What takes people in the two opposing directions of street-dweller and millionaire? We were all at primary school together as equals, sitting side by side in class, weren't we?

The rich tapestry of life is so exciting, even though it can sometimes be terrifying at the same time.

Early June 2003

Feeling quite numb, I packed up and left my beautiful rented apartment a couple of weeks ago. Peter, an old school friend I hadn't seen for years, took me and some of my stuff to a squat. It's dirty, dingy, and sunless compared with the beautiful apartment by the river, but I'm grateful for a roof over my head and cold water for showering.

I went to see the Salvation Army financial counselor, who couldn't help much. He said my strength and outlook would see me through.

How does he know that? What can he see in me that I fail to see in myself right now?

Late June 2003

There's a big hole in the floor, so I use it as a seat. I sit on the floor with my legs through the hole and my feet on the ground below to eat my dinner. It's nice to have somewhere to sit and it's nice to have something to eat. I half expected a mouse to pop its dear little nose up and ask to share my dinner. I would appreciate the company.

I sent thank you cards to friends who have been so kind to me in various ways.

NOW

Now, nearly ten years later, I look back at the growth I've achieved from that difficult time. I think about how some people end up living life on the streets and how I knew that I wouldn't. How did the Salvation Army counselor know that, too? What did he see in me that made him say I'd be fine? Somehow I must have exuded a sense of hope.

I recall that my thought-tape at that time was a continual loop of "I'm not good enough, I don't deserve..., I can't afford...." Through reading many books and listening to positive tapes, I was able to recognize my negative thoughts and learn to catch myself thinking them. I practiced replacing those thoughts with new positive ones, and recited an affirmation every time I became aware of my thoughts. I would sing the words and dance around, adding, "Thank you, thank you, thank you" for everything I could think of. "Thank you for the trees and sunny day, for my healthy body, my family, and many precious friends."

I kept an old cassette recorder with me and left it running when I went to sleep. Even during those toughest times I listened to tapes of Dr. Wayne Dyer's comforting and loving messages, as well as Robert Kiyosaki's discussions about financial freedom. I tried so hard to believe it could be possible for me to turn my life around, and I never stopped believing in a better future. I worked at recognizing and replacing the deep-rooted beliefs that caused those negative thoughts.

The main thing I needed to do was forgive. There were other people involved, and we had made a joint venture agreement that went wrong. I could have sued them and held a grudge. Instead I sent love and forgiveness every time I thought of them. Yes, that was extremely difficult. I took full responsibility for my own decisions and where they had led me.

I kept a loving and open heart, and tried always to search for the best in every person and circumstance, to stay grateful for the small things. That's evident now as I look back on my journals. The intervening years would have been completely different without that experience, and I'm very grateful for where it has led me.

Today I'm living my dream, looking out over snow-capped mountains, listening to native birds and the babbling mountain stream. I'm about to purchase a glorious, sunny apartment, after ten years spent working very hard to pull myself out of that quagmire and repay the debt. I stayed focused, believed in a positive future, and here I am, sitting in the sun, eating my favorite chocolate, just because I can, and crying tears of pure joy and gratitude for my life and where it's brought me.

Don't be afraid to sample the smorgasbord of life. Have a go. Be willing to stretch your boundaries. Remember that the depths of adversity are matched by the highs of joy. Universal love is the balance of what we perceive as "good" and "bad." It's the total mix of life's ups and downs. Life is not always a bed of roses. It's sometimes a fast-flowing, muddy river. Just keep on believing in yourself and never stop work-ing towards your dream. I know at times it seems totally impossible, but you can do it. Trust and learn to enjoy the exciting roller coaster that is your life.

The smorgasbord of life called Jane St Catherine is from a secure sub-urban existence. Leaving her husband and an office job, she set off on an old 250cc trail bike to ride around the world. With determination and courage, she has overcome many challenges. Continually learn-ing from diverse experiences, Jane has worked in Parliament House and on prawn trawlers, driven massive mining trucks, and taught chil-dren on outback Australian cattle stations. Connect with Jane at www. JaneStCatherine.com.au.

Wake-Up Calls for Family Leadership

Jens Erik Hoverby, MSc

The Killing

IN THE HEART OF COPENHAGEN, my girlfriend Ida and I were sitting opposite two female sex therapists. I was blaming Ida for rejecting sex with me for most of six years. Aggressively I said, "I can't forgive you for robbing me of my sexual identity and self-esteem!" Immediately they interrupted me. "Jens Erik, can you forgive yourself for letting her do that?"

That question stabbed me like a knife in my gut and left me absolutely speechless. I was the victim of Ida's rejection! She hurt me. How could my pain be my own fault? This wake-up call turned my world upside down. The maps and recipes I had been handed to navigate my life proved to be wrong. My foundational beliefs about the world and myself as a man started dying.

New Maps and Recipes

Once a wise man told me, "If things do not turn out the way you expected them to, it's because there is something you do not understand"! So what didn't I understand? What did I need to learn from my experience with Ida?

For the following seventeen years, I chose a path of learning to rewrite my maps and recipes. As bad habits tend to pass down through generations, one essential question has followed me all these years: "How can I help others and my own kids NOT to fall into the same trap?"

I hope to inspire you with an answer to this question, which became clearer through a series of wake-up experiences.

Felt Like a Loser

I had just turned thirty and was rich in everything but inner peace. My master's exam grades were very high, but I was ashamed of having spent three times the scheduled time to finish. My fight for a reputation for being the best came at a very high price. I felt worthless, inferior, alone, socially ill, and envious of other's success. At gatherings in the presence of friends and family, I politely faked a smile. "I feel great, thank you, and you?" Inside my body every cell screamed, "I am a failure, worthless, and a fake." I'd withdraw early to recuperate in bed. Luckily nobody noticed – or did they?

A new recipe had to give me peace from my self-terror and an answer to "Who am I?"

Learning That I Am a Peaceful Soul

My search brought me to Brahma Kumaris Spiritual University – a place to learn how to manifest inner peace and higher consciousness through meditation. I had always thought of myself as my body, thoughts, and emotions, but my teacher said, "Jens Erik, we see you as neither. For us you are a soul who chooses your body, thoughts, and emotions. Your core is already peaceful. You achieve peace by letting go of the disturbing thoughts and emotions you don't want." This mindset resonated with me and helped me take full responsibility for the heartache of my inferiority and Ida's rejections years earlier.

Through meditation I learned not to become a victim by letting others disturb and annoy me. I can now choose which events to react to, as well as when and how. This is the essence of self-leadership. However, listening to others was still not my strong side. This came clear in my next wake-up call.

Learning To Be Vulnerable and Listen with My Heart

I fell in a deep love with Sif, and two years later we merged our soul partnership into marriage. I felt 100 percent sure that our two souls were meant for each other – for life. But on our way to our honeymoon, I learned that eternal love has its price.

We fought and quarreled on the way to the airport, in the plane, in the bus, and on the ferry. "You are not listening!" she cried. "No, you are not listening!" I shouted. After twelve hours of verbal combat, I lay down alone with my closed eyes on a bench in the sun. "What a bitch!" I thought. "How can I open her mind to listen?" And when the cramps of anger evaporated, I asked myself, "I obviously get nowhere trying to change Sif. What do I not understand? What do I need to learn?"

At that exact moment I woke up and was ready to grow up some more. Immediately I texted my best friend who married us, saying,

"Jesper, help me save my marriage. Just get me into the non-violent communications class starting next month."

For eighteen months, daily I practiced empathetic listening and communicating my observations, vulnerable emotions, needs, and suggestions for action. This not only changed the way I thought and acted, it literally had a strong healing effect. Indirectly, Marshall B. Rosenberg, who wrote the book *Nonviolent Communication: A Language of Life*, helped save my marriage.

Learning That I Am Masculine Love That Penetrates with an Open Heart

I understood my own needs better now, but apparently I was not reading Sif's needs clearly. In a conversation with her, she shouted desperately, "I need a MAN!"

At the time I worked as a self-employed life coach, but my business did not take off, and I needed unemployment support. She was patient for the first twenty months, and then she started shouting. The first time I ignored her, because I refused to take the full responsibility for providing for our family, but the second time I was ready to listen and take action. My friend Jesper invited me to join him and seven other ambitious men who wanted to grow into "superior men," and this turned out to be the best and most transforming thing I have ever done for myself.

David Deida's book *The Way of the Superior Man* was our "bible." Once a week I met them to coach and be coached on living my purpose at work and taking full masculine responsibility for my wife's trust and desire for me. This turned out to be a tough ambition.

I grew up in the shadow side of the masculine power, where men cover up their fears and insecurity, and because I was criticized for behaving like my father, I doubted and hated the man in myself. Therefore, despite my self-development efforts, I still felt socially alienated from most men in my network, and had a hard time taking advice from other men. Not the easiest starting point for a "superior man."

One week I failed to do my daily notes that the group challenged me to do. Instead I covered up the truth and presented my notebook as if I had completed the challenge correctly. "Jens Erik, are you faking us?" they asked. "Yes," I admitted, and felt deeply ashamed for not trusting them with my truth. I also felt relief, because hiding the embarrassing truth had consumed a lot of my energy.

Some meetings later I came unprepared again. This time I told them the naked truth and that I felt afraid, guilty, and inferior. My experience with men told me to expect the group's judgmental disappointment, but it didn't happen. They just smiled with warm compassion and said, "Congratulations. You came unprepared, but finally we feel you. You are honest and authentic with us. Thank you."

After this wake-up experience, I finally dropped my loser attitude – "I am always right about what's best for me" – and started taking the group's advice seriously.

Understanding What I Did Wrong

What did I do that caused me to end up unsuccessful and unhappy in sex therapy? I was at war with myself and turned my greatest strengths against myself. My soul has a talent for architecting visionary ideals and the highest potential for excellence. I see it fast and I am passionate about it. However, on the shadow side I can become indecisive and judge non-perfection harshly.

From very young, I systematically criticized my own talents and became greedy and jealous of personal qualities and qualifications that others possessed. This became a lethal disease that almost killed me with sadness, envy, and shame. These emotions are now history, because wise, compassionate people helped me love my inner light and my shadow side. Now I can say:

I live to light up the path for others to see.
I need friends who see the light I was born to be,
and I value the light in all living, as much as in me.

I believe this is what we are all here to learn and to teach others. So let's pass on the wisdom to the leaders of tomorrow.

Inspire Family Leadership

When we look at the bigger picture, both our ecological and economic systems are way out of balance, and we are indebted for decades into our children's future. Our values of governance are heading for a major wake-up call. We seriously need a new generation of leaders who can see themselves and our world as one organism, and who understand that any organism at war with itself is doomed. We need enlightened leaders who make others grow and shine in greatness.

Therefore, dear parents, teachers, coaches, managers, and even politicians, let's join in a quest to teach the leaders of tomorrow how to take on that leadership.

Let's ask them about their vision and support them in realizing it. Ask them how they feel and what they need. Find them a school that doesn't judge them on the same scale, but coaches them to experience the power of their passions and talents, and to see them in others.

Say, "I love your soul as it is – don't change."

And most important, be the role model they need. For this may well be the biggest pebble we can ever throw in their pond.

Jens Erik Hoverby, is a Leadership Coach and award winning essay author. He lives his dream with his wife and two sons in Malta, south of Italy, from where he is founding a Global Family Leadership Academy. If you want to contribute to this mission or you want to become part of the global community of parents that take their family to new heights, then sign up at www.TransformationCompany.com.

Surrender to Love

Judy Guadalupe

AHH, THE WAY WE HUMANS GROW and awaken. The most powerful opportunities to grow and change in my life have often come in unplanned ways. Have you had a few twists and turns on your way? Bruce Lipton writes about these times of great change and transformation occurring in our world. He speaks of "imaginal cells" – those first cells within the caterpillar's chrysalis that realize themselves to be butterflies.

As you and I allow ourselves to be transparent and vulnerable, we heal and uncover our authentic selves – our essence of love. Our transformation is like an imaginal cell for the planet – a pebble in the pond. The ripples help others realize their butterfly potential. The death of something is always simultaneously met with new birth. Have you experienced that your most profound transformation often occurs through the greatest challenges or upheavals in your life? I sure have.

Often, it seems, the time of metamorphosis between caterpillar and butterfly is fraught with challenge and pain. Yet as we surrender resistance, the love essence within all life is forever unraveling itself.

I have been blessed again and again to see that moving through pain and trusting what I cannot yet see will yield unforeseen blessings and growth. I wish this for you, wherever you find yourself as you read these stories: that you let go and let God as you say yes to the wings stirring upon your back.

I'll start my story at the beginning. In 1960, into Planet Earth I came. Born to a beautiful family of a variety of forms of "godlove," I learned many lessons as the third child of seven in New York going to Catholic school. At the time of this writing, my parents have twenty-two grandchildren and three great-grandchildren — forty-something of us in total. I would need to write a series of books to speak to the pebbles in my family who add to the transformation of this world through love.

As a young child, I was quite sensitive. I talked to the walls and sucked my thumb, daydreaming for hours on end. I have some memory of connecting with my friends of light, but little by little the connection faded. Growing up, I liked people, could feel how they felt, and wanted to help them feel better.

I was not a fan of school, and thus school was not a fan of me. As I grew, the "not good enough" syndrome caught onto my thoughts like a virus, and the aspect of me that was becoming all I knew myself to be started to believe it. Others had better grades and seemed to do life better than I. This translated into belief systems that I was inadequate, weird, incapable, and didn't belong here. Like many, the light of my essence began to dim. I felt deeply, and took on the feelings of those around me, not knowing how to use my empathic abilities.

In high school, my friends and I were kindhearted beings who loved to party and rebel against some norm we could not access or fit into. Soon the low self-esteem and wanting to feel different or "get the hell outta here" plagues took hold. Mixed with guilt and shame from inherited lineages we all share, I disconnected from myself and the gifts I've come to share. I decided, like many at the time, to self-medicate. By the end of high school, I had no conscious access to my inner world or spirit.

After that, life went downhill fast. I spent eight years trying to get it together – back to school, new cities, new relationships, and alone in the closet with a pipe. The power of addiction had taken hold.

As love would have it, at twenty-six, after three sleepless nights on yet another freebase binge, I needed to get home. At the risk of sounding cliché, this is how love called me home: In front of my parent's church, I had to pull over as my eyes were burning and I was unable to see. I remember thinking I was going blind. Not knowing what to do, I declared, "Dear God, if you do not make me blind, I will do anything." Soon after, my eyes cleared and I drove home. My mother, a huge rock in my pond, shared that she simultaneously told God, "I give up. I give her to You. There is nothing I can do anymore. She is Yours."

Within a couple of days I was in rehab. Within a couple of weeks I desired a new life. I was immediately graced with people who had something that I wanted. I could taste it, this light in their eyes, and I listened.

My counselor recommended a halfway house, and I knew it was a gift. For some, living in a house with fourteen recently addicted women, going to meetings, counseling, and working may not be seen as a gift. Not always easy, but love called me inward and forward. I stayed a year.

My true self underneath the self-loathing, guilt, and doubts was emerging. One evening on a run, I stopped at a lake and sat on the ground. Within seconds I felt as if I were disappearing, and I could feel myself as one with the water, the birds, and the trees. It was as if I were melting and expanding at the same time. There was no fear, just vast peace and timeless love. As my awareness came back to my body, my heart felt like it had blasted open. I ran home. I spoke with my counselor, who referred me to the other residents' counselor, Sister Jane, a Catholic nun, for the "spiritual stuff." I felt some resistance, but agreed to meet.

The evening boasted a gentle breeze, and the white wicker chairs on the porch of my temporary five-floor Victorian home shone in the moonlight as we sat. Forever etched upon my soul, we communed. We spoke of love, God, other lives, and her friend who channeled – some concepts that I'd never entertained, yet were deeply familiar. This friend told Sister Jane that anyone who came to Sister Jane would move toward the light. Sister Jane is a pebble in the pond of hundreds of women imbued with addiction and other life challenges who encounter a path of awakening. United Way did a documentary about this house called Where the Walls Breathe Love.

I found it funny when I asked her, "How about the part in church when you say 'Lord, I am not worthy to receive you'? I feel unworthy enough. I don't understand this." She smiled her brilliant-eyed smile and said, "Oh, I skip that part."

We spoke well into the night. Her presence drew me, the soul of love I am, into the present moment. I knew and felt God in me and everything. I realized that the rest of my life would be guided by this mystery, this power of love called God by some, and that I was totally and completely supported. It was the journey of a lifetime, the true reason I exist, emerging. Love calls forth love, and this is what she did for us.

As love heals, compassion blooms, and this led me to become an addictions counselor. With the impulse of awakening as my guide, books fell off shelves and teachers appeared at the right moments. Learning and sharing the deep and powerful teachings that support recovery was a grace-filled blessing.

Before long I met my partner of twenty-two years, my being danced as we met, experiencing the timeless connection of our souls. We have three magnificent children, each child calling forth more of my true self to heal and show up more fully. Being a partner and parent has offered me the most profound experiences of loving, as well as the unparalleled opportunities for healing and growth. If you know any of these wise old souls in children's bodies, you know how good they are at calling you home, pushing the buttons to bring up any impostor less than love showing up in your life! Over the years, I found myself to be most challenged to translate what I experience in the silent space of love into the physical world and my relationships. Ask my family — they can tell you!

As life moved forward through challenges and triumphs, resistance and surrender, contraction and expansion, I explored and studied as I uncovered the gifts I have come to share. Now as a writer, spiritual counselor/coach, and inspirer for the soul, I love supporting others in discovering how love is endlessly unraveling itself in their lives.

Have you ever been addicted, or are you finding yourself in the grip of an addiction now? Be gentle, and ask for help. Your inner wisdom may create crisis to bring you home to love. We can become addicted to many things, looking for God in all the wrong places. An addiction, when addressed, is often the catalyst that takes us from looking outside ourselves to looking within and accessing the inner peace and love that we are. The most magnificent "high" comes from the realization of our full and utter connection with our Source.

Together we have the unprecedented opportunity to realize our individualized wholeness while experiencing this mysterious, unified field of love that connects us all. How thrilling to be part of the global transformation as we hear many more stories of how we surrender to love, one pebble at a time.

Judy Guadalupe is a spiritual life counselor and intuitive for individuals, parents, and families. She hosts and teaches transformational classes and presents evenings of humor and inspirational word that invite laughter into the transformation process. Judy is owner and manager of the Creative Healing & Arts Center, and presents at Children of the New Earth Conferences and Seeding the Future Now, which supports the emergence of new schools around the globe. To receive her free offer, visit www.JudyGuadalupe.com/pebbles-book-bonus.

Unraveling

Kimberly Barclay, MA

AS I REFLECTED ON MY LIFE in preparation for the message I was to bring to this book, I was reminded of how small steps and persever-ance can create a life so filled with beauty it is almost unrecognizable. My heart is so wide open and I feel truly blessed to be on earth at this time in this amazing way.

Out of the darkness comes the greatest light.

My commitment to begin a spiritual journey of self-discovery and healing was a catalyst for change. Prior to that time, my primary goal in life was to escape. A part of me did NOT want to continue this human experience. I felt lost, broken, and completely disconnected from my Soul. I avoided the pain in my heart built up from many dis-appointments, misunderstandings, and misperceptions. Denial is such an amazing coping mechanism of the ego, and my ego was a "master of denial."

Proficient at being "the good girl" who was friendly, responsible, an honor student, and a diligent worker, I also had a strong "rebel archetype," rebelling against life, myself, and the pain in my heart through excessive eating, smoking, and drinking — always ready and prepared to fight if necessary.

Many times I would look at myself in the mirror while intoxicated or feeling out of control, and ask myself, "WHY? Why are you doing what you don't want to do? Why are you so miserable and unhappy?" In the reflection I would momentarily connect with a deep, truthful part of myself whose presence would slip through my fingertips, eventually returning as a permanent guiding force directing me to wake up, face the truth, and get real.

Courageously, I began telling the truth to myself and expressing my truth to others — adopting a consistent quality of open, authentic expression in each moment, no matter what. Layers upon layers of masks and denial began to unravel with each authentically spoken word, opening my eyes to astounding revelations about myself and my life, previously unseen.

Somehow my masterful ego had shielded me for many years from seeing an obvious truth which perpetuated the disconnection from my Soul. As the veil of illusion was lifted, I could no longer suppress or deny having an addiction to alcohol. With sincere humility, I admitted I was not strong enough to conquer this on my own and needed help. Within a few months, I checked myself into a thirty-day rehab facility and started a detoxification process, affecting me physically, mentally, emotionally, and spiritually.

In time, I began to feel alive again and reconnect to my life in a whole new way. My newfound energy was channeled into getting somewhere, achieving recognition, or obtaining the ideal possession to convince myself that I truly mattered. While desperately searching for yet another opportunity, a poem I had written years prior suddenly came into my awareness.

The future is just a moment away
Forever moving, forever in front of me
Just until I can breathe again
Just until my obstacles are cleared

I am desperately trying to plan for the future
The ever changing unknown destination
Will it ever be known?
Will I ever be able to plan?

For that is the question of the moment
Then the moment is gone
The questions come again
The moment is gone again

Where did all the moments go?
Planning, analyzing, and trying to figure everything out
But I cannot forget that the moments never return
The truth is, that somewhere among the midst,
The future became the present.

I realized I was bypassing my precious life by planning and living for the future — missing everyday moments that truly mattered, seeing now how my protective ego instinctively knew that if I were to totally stop I would uncover deeper truths that would lead to greater changes.

I intended to return to the "magical child archetype" I once embodied, who saw beauty and was fully engaged in each sacred moment. With this intention, a deeper layer of repressed issues surfaced, culminating in a beautiful acceptance of hidden aspects of myself.

As the tears started to fall
What began to disappear was an amazing wall
Created to stop the emotions from flowing
Behind that wall were the parts that stopped growing
The part afraid of getting hurt
A part that was quiet and could not be heard
The part that felt weak and insecure
A part that was also so very very pure

As the tears started to fall
I realized the crumbling of the wall
That not only blocked my pain from showing
It also stopped my light from glowing
I opened my heart and love poured out
I opened my heart and was able to shout
I opened my heart to the world and its glory
And realized in an instant it was only a story
I had believed without knowing the grandest picture
Without knowing who I was or what could make my life richer

I opened up to a whole new world inside
And declared to myself "I no longer have to hide."
This path I'm choosing allows me to be free
Allows me to let go and allows me to be
Be true to the moment as the rest has subsided
And feel the joy that, inside me, has always resided

In hindsight, my life makes absolute sense. I now see perfection, divinity, and Truth, with clarity and compassion. Gratefully, during the journey of unraveling, it was revealed that I was NOT broken. I discovered I was a product of the human condition – the collective "egoic" consciousness energetically existing on earth. I understood how desperate human beings can be to escape, and how we can become so disconnected from Truth. I saw how undeniably strong the "saboteur archetype" is at resisting change, and how every human act, at the core, is primarily motivated by freedom and/or love or the lack thereof.

We all fundamentally want the same thing. We are all connected and can fully understand each other when we open our hearts to understanding, compassion, Truth, and this amazingly intricate human experience which encompasses both light and dark.

Reflections of the Soul open the heart.

Letting go opened a channel through which insights flowed into my awareness. My heartfelt intention is for you to be inspired and/or re-minded as I share them with you.

Your life happens in each precious, simple, exquisite, and expansive moment. There is no rewind. There is no second chance to get your moments back. Staying connected to each moment is an eternal gift we give ourselves that actually ripples out energetically.

You are always being guided by your Soul. Tuning in to the channel of divine guidance is possible for everyone. With complete surrender, it becomes the most consistent and strongest guiding system of our lives, leading us perfectly and attracting synchronicity beyond logic. By following intuitive nudges and taking each divinely revealed step, one step at a time, life unfolds like a plush, red carpet. What transpires from that space of openness and receptivity is much larger than our imagination can conceive.

As one surrenders, Truth is revealed.

Living in Truth means shining light into darkness, facing the ego's misperceived reality of suffering, embracing it, and, in that space, transmuting it. If old memories or wounds surface, accepting them with open arms and unconditional love for what they represent creates a space for healing and integration. When you don't resist what is, you are truly free. When we accept all of life and open our hearts to the present and current reality, we rise above perceived obstacles, limitations, past conditioning, and future concerns, creating a whole new world.

From that energy, life becomes an amazing adventure and a cherished gift. The future is exciting, yet paradoxically, there is no need for anything, because being immersed in the present moment is enough, and everything else becomes icing on the cake. The unknown is embraced. Trust and faith become inherent in "beingness."

Risks are no longer seen as risks. They become liberating leaps into the spaciousness of life itself, allowing you to soar. With each leap, our wings become stronger, and the wind beneath them, fueled by faith and supported by surrender, becomes incredibly apparent.

Only when we surrender to the unknown will the known become possible.

Humans are actually comprised of a "split being," each part amazingly able to live in two completely different simultaneous realities – the ego's reality and the soul's reality. Whatever reality you give energy to, you strengthen. A "spiritual warrior" is one who sees both realities while consciously navigating the journey, transferring energy from the ego to the Soul.

The "**G.A.M.E.** of Life" unconsciously played out by humanity is **G**oing **A**long **M**erged with the **E**go. A conscious "**G.A.M.E.**" we can intentionally participate in to align with our soul and embark on a spiritual warrior's journey is **G**iving the **A**uthentic-Self (the Soul) **M**ore **E**nergy. I encourage you to give energy to YOUR Soul where 100 percent presence, surrender, freedom, love, peace, and joy reside.

As we feed our Souls and our intuition becomes louder, our energy is freed for full engagement in each moment. LIFE itself becomes MORE than enough. Through that energy we attract amazing circumstances and begin to live in a miraculous **F.L.O.W.** – **F**inally **L**etting go of the **O**utside **W**orld. Positive and magical synchronicity floods our human experience and becomes a natural way of LIFE.

It takes a Spiritual Warrior to unlearn all that has been learned and undo all that has been done.

Kimberly Barclay, MA is a spiritual mentor, certified life coach, inspirational speaker, and founder of Moment Connections. She has a master's degree in spiritual psychology and is fascinated with the human experience and passionate in assisting those who are truly ready to reconnect to Truth and live fully engaged in LIFE through understanding the ego and the Authentic-Self (the Soul). Email her at Kimberly@ MomentConnections.com for a comprehensive comparison entitled "The Ego vs. The Authentic-Self." For more information, visit www. MomentConnections.com.

The Eyes Observing Your World

Kimberly Burnham, PhD

THE FORCE OF THE ACCIDENT IS STILL in Joanne's small face as I gently rest my hands over her cool, sleeping eyes. I connect with the vibration – the energy – the crunch of the cold metal bumper as a car slides through the red light into the crosswalk, slamming into her stroller, shattering bones. I feel inadequate as I coach myself, "I am here to guide this three-year-old's healing. All of my training, all of my skills, have brought me to this day. I can do this!"

"I don't know how you're going to do it," says my boss, the creative and clinical force behind a large natural-medicine clinic. "But your job is to fix up the bone bruises, the micro-fractures in the back of the orbit of her eyes." This mandate affects me personally as a human being desiring the love and respect of others, and wanting to contribute to health solutions, hope, and peace in the world. Professionally, it challenges me as an Integrative Manual Therapist to further develop my hands-on skills and facilitate vitality in people with challenges in the area of vision and brain health.

Alternative medicine practitioners are often told what we can't do, what we can't diagnose, what isn't possible. And yet I have been privileged to see miracles on a regular basis.

On this day, I use my hands to change the quality of a life, for this little girl, perhaps for the next 100 years. The damage is extensive, but her mother believes in me. Her father expects me to succeed using my hands, my heart, and my awareness to shift the energy and effects of the trauma. And so I do. In this moment nothing is impossible. I participate in and witness the gift of a child's sight returned. Over time, much of the damage to her face heals, and I am reminded of Mark Nepo's cancer recovery story in *The Book of Awakening,* in which he shares, "Like most gifts, it is the passing of something meaningful between people that awakens us to our potential." You also have the potential to heal and share what you see along the journey with loved ones.

Interpreting Visual Reality

Your potential is deeply impacted by the way you see. Albert Einstein said, "The most important decision we make is whether we believe we live in a friendly or hostile Universe." What do you choose? This transformative day with Joanne, I chose a supportive Universe, in which I can see with my eyes and my external sight, and feel with my hands an inner vision of all the possibilities.

My own journey to better eye health did not begin in my twenties when I was diagnosed with keratoconus, a genetic eye condition characterized by severe light sensitivity and rupturing corneas. I didn't know there was anything that could be done. I didn't yet know I could do anything. In my forties, after receiving manual therapy treatment, I looked through my glasses, confused, thinking I had picked up someone else's. Then I understood: my vision could change. And this realization shifted my view of my potential and the healing capacity of others forever.

Perhaps, like me, you have been diagnosed with a genetic condition or an autoimmune dysfunction, chronic migraine pain, fatigue, or a nervous system imbalance. Perhaps you have also been told there is nothing that can be done, but your eyes are designed to see and inform your brain about the magnificent richness in this world. For me, following up with hours of self-care, hands-on healing for my own eyes, healthy eating, and the continued exploration of inner shamanic images has steadily improved my vision. It is myth that your vision will incessantly deteriorate as you age.

Now, at the age of fifty-four, I have better vision than I did at forty, and no migraines. In fact, I probably have better sight than when I was twelve and started wearing glasses! The secret I share with my coaching clients is that each moment I can change how I see and what I listen to. You can, too.

Awareness Is the Key

You are a powerful being, and with a radio you can listen to music being played miles away, but how you interpret sound or enjoy it depends on many factors.

Has someone created a working radio?
Do you believe a radio is useful in your life?
Are you listening?
Can you differentiate between sound and noise?
Do you respond to sounds in a way that supports your learning, creativity, and contribution?

Answers to these questions influence the usefulness of sound waves, but none of them influence their existence or the information they carry. No one but you knows how exactly how you will do it, but your job is to see the world in a way that serves and empowers you to truly experience the opportunities and miracles all around you, because, I guarantee, they are there. Miracles are everywhere. Are you seeing them? Do you hear them?

What you can learn from the experiences of others is that you have a choice. You can pay attention to what you feel, and lay down bright, new, healthy connections in your brain like Jack:

Agitated, Jack says, "I can't tell the difference between red and orange. My eyes jiggle when I jump up and down like this." A six-year-old, Jack crashed his face into a chain-link fence two days earlier. The swelling and inflammation is causing too much fluid around his eyes. They jiggle and irritate the nerves that carry color information to his brain. After a couple of hours of acupressure-like therapy, he is vigorously hopping, exclaiming, "My eyes don't jiggle anymore!" Within a week he has reclaimed his rich and vibrant Universe. When I speak to groups, I share this story because it illustrates how easily nerves can heal.

What if it is just that easy? What if you can increase the vibrancy of your world by putting one hand over your eyes and the other hand on a reflex point, for example, an "Integrative Manual Therapy" synchronizer at the hard tip of the left elbow, or a point at the back of the neck along the gallbladder meridian? These reflex points can be touched, pressed, or rubbed, and then connected with the eyes for a few minutes to enhance your potential. Is it worth trying to see, literally, if you can use your hands and mind to heal your brain?

In addition to the structure of your eyes, what you focus on influences the quality of your vision. Brain science shows that it is easier for your mind to strive for what you desire than to let go of what you don't want. What do you want more of? If truly anything can shift concerning your health, life, or relationships, what do you want? How does "better" look and feel?

Pebbles of Independence

Does "better" feel like independence? Do you worry about your vision as you age? A few years ago, a client was going blind with macular degeneration. At eighty-two years old, Janice was afraid of losing her ability to read and drive. Basically, she was anxious about losing her independence. On a budget, she could afford about one hour of hands-on treatment per month, plus self-care exercises. Almost magically, at Janice's next six-month checkup, the ophthalmologist said, "There has been no deterioration or worsening of your vision." She herself reports that colors, like the autumn yellow of Colorado aspen trees, are brighter. She feels comfortable driving on winding mountain roads. She embodies the Nicaraguan saying, "Eyes that see, do not grow old."

Marie, one of my favorite clients, had a dual diagnosis of optic neuritis, or nerve inflammation, and multiple sclerosis, an autoimmune disease in which brain and spine cells are not properly recognized. Returning to her doctor for another insurance-covered massage therapy prescription, she was arrogantly told, "The optic neuritis is so much better, you should just be happy with the results." With enviable spunk she replied, "I am happy. I am just not satisfied." Don't you think this is an awesome approach to life, one in which you recognize and truly see the nested fractal patterns of your life, where everything is related and connected? Look for ways to create a life in which you recognize the familiar and strive to learn and understand the unfamiliar. After all, eyes are eyes, and whether they are young or old, trauma impacted or diseased, eyes, brains, and hearts can all transform.

If you drop a shiny, smooth pebble of information into the flow of energy moving through your eyes and through your nervous system, where is this knowledge attracted to? Where is the information needed? Which areas of your being are sustained by a more conscious connection with your eyes? Which areas would transform with the nutritional exchange they need? Where is the smartest, most-connected part of your nervous system?

There. What did you just think of? What does that part have to share that will transform your well-being and create the vision you want, now that you know what is possible? Be open to your own magical intuition — to your inner nerve whisperer. Find the way these solutions transform you and your world. Cause a ripple in the pond.

Visit www.KimberlyBurnham.com for additional healing stories: a twelve-year-old girl overcoming a lazy eye or a friendly, ferocious-looking Rottweiler's eye injury, and revitalization in individuals with autism, Huntington's, Parkinson's, MS, and fibromyalgia. Explore secrets found in *The Nerve Whisperer: Recover Your Life through Brain Health*. Enhance your journey with effective self-care exercises, Matrix Energetics guidance, fractal images, and Information Medicine training videos. Tap the "Morphic Field" of vision healing. Share your discoveries and these free resources with a loved one.

Life Is a Hoot If We'd Only Laugh

Lilia Shoshanna Rae

I TAKE LIFE SERIOUSLY. I am determined to get it right. I have studied a gazillion courses and read two gazillion books to find the magic formula.

And I have to laugh, because most of what we need to know is so simple. Why do we complicate it so?

Rule Number One: Breathe.

We breathe every moment we live in these earthly bodies. Yet how often do we forget that we need only bring awareness to the breath to find more peace in our lives?

Simply focusing on our breath brings us to a place inside where peace resides – the "peace that passes understanding" that connects us to the Divine in all of creation, including ourselves.

I have to confess that I am writing this as much for myself as for any reader. I keep forgetting this simple fact!

A case in point: I just helped to organize a weekend with a world-renowned author and leader of meditations. Key to his method of meditation is merely focusing on the breath and letting the attention relax, allowing us to drop into that inner world that is always there.

For two days, as we practiced meditating in this simple way, I found it easy to drop into a peaceful place, letting my attention relax, becoming aware of what is always there. It felt euphoric.

Three days later, I was back to focusing on the challenges in my life – meeting deadlines, learning new computer skills to get my message out to the world, and keeping up with email and Facebook postings that seem to grow exponentially. I lost the feeling of euphoria. Instead, I felt a two-ton brick of anxiety in my heart where blissful peace had been so present.

I had forgotten to breathe. I used a guided visualization to help me recover because I was so stuck in that anxious energy. It took a while, and a few other breathing techniques, but I got myself back to that place of ease.

So I invite you in this moment as you read these words to take your awareness to your breath. Follow it for just a few cycles. Inhale. Exhale. Just a few times, following it completely through each cycle. How does that feel? We all know this works, but sometimes it helps to have a reminder. Just breathe.

Rule Number Two: Begin from Beingness

Our breath leads us to a sense of our "Beingness" – to who we are without the trappings of our conditioning. We remember that we are part of the Whole, and the Whole is divine creation. We are one divine spark of light and love within "All That Is." We don't need to comprehend what that means. We need only to open up to the experience of it.

As we act from that place of Beingness, we know that we do what we were born to do. It is why we came into this particular human body – not our neighbor's body, or one from a previous lifetime. We came into this particular vessel at this time to live a particular purpose with particular gifts. Acting on purpose brings our light and love into the world. Our divine spark glows and grows.

Yet we often forget to connect to our Beingness. Remember the day I felt a two-ton brick in my heart? I had forgotten to breathe and stay aware. I allowed myself to believe that it was my human self alone facing the challenges. Of course I became anxious! Once I centered myself and connected to that place of Beingness, I knew I was not alone. I felt supported by the Universe, and at peace.

Rule Number Three: Laughter Is Key

There are times, though, when I get so stuck in my emotions that I feel disconnected from my Beingness, and focusing on my breath does not work. I feel so overcome with feelings that I have trouble shifting to a higher vibration.

Yesterday is a prime example. I left my house early to meet my son at his college to go with him to traffic court, giving myself plenty of time under normal circumstances. As soon as I pulled away from my house, though, all I could see were red and white lights in every direction. It was a gridlock on the streets at that still-dark, early hour. I kept going because I felt it was important for me to be there. I knew my son could handle it on his own, but my motherly nature insisted that I be there for him. I hoped that the sea of lights would clear and let me sail smoothly through to be by his side.

That did not happen. After thirty minutes of going fifteen miles per hour instead of fifty-five, I called my son and told him he needed to go by himself, and I would try to get there as soon as I could. He was cool with that. I was not.

I found myself tensing up, worrying about what would happen if I were not there. Catching myself in this downward spiral, I focused on my breath. It helped a little, but the tension was still quite present. I started using energy medicine and tapping techniques with one of my hands.

Still, that did not shift my energy. I kept making wrong turns and getting lost.

Finally, I began to laugh. It was too absurd to take seriously any more. I was not going to be on time, and there was nothing I could do about it. As soon as I started laughing, my anxiety broke. I was no longer tight and tense. I was relaxed and going with (the very slow) flow. Laughter came to my rescue in this rather mundane but common life situation. It is essential to be able to laugh to get through our more difficult challenges.

For me, prosperity is my biggest challenge, and I know I am not alone. To make a shift in my prosperity consciousness, I took a class this summer. However, I began to balk when I found that it required tithing to my church. I don't know about you, but tithing strikes terror in my heart. It was only for ten weeks, so I decided to try it as an experiment.

When I started the class, I had very little income. I had used up much of my savings as I had switched careers to teach classes on mystery school topics and build my intuitive healing practice. I'd written a book on my spiritual awakening and was working toward getting it published. It looked like it was going to take years to earn enough to support myself in this new work.

What I learned in the class was that tithing is a part of the "Universal Law of Sufficiency and Abundance" – the law that teaches us that there is enough in the Universe for everyone to be prosperous, and that we show our trust in the Universe by giving back to our source of inspiration.

That makes sense to me. There is a natural flow to the Universe, and we are asked to participate in that flow, but it takes trust. And that is when I had to face up to a hard truth. I did not trust the Universe! Instead, I had been trying to rewrite its Universal Laws!

Seeing myself in the stark light of hard truth, I had to laugh. How could I not trust the Divine, the All That Is? How could I not see that the Universal Laws are designed to help us work in harmony with the Divine? Once I could laugh, my whole being lightened up. I decided to be a full partner with the Universe.

After making this commitment, I received a phone call asking me to return to my former work on a part-time basis. I also received a free session with a fabulous business coach who is helping me structure my work to bring in the income I need from the work I feel called to do. Both were vital contributions to my sense of prosperity.

Of greatest value was the gift of peace of mind I learned from this experiment. The Universe has my back and I now know it. There is no price tag to place on that sense of peace. I also received the reminder of the gift of laughter. If I can laugh at what I am taking so seriously, particularly if I make it a deep belly laugh, my emotions shift, my perceptions shift, and my whole life shifts.

I have not achieved all of my financial goals… yet. Prosperity is a path of learning for me, but I would not trade my peace of mind for a whole boatload of gold bullion (tempting as that might be).

I end this writing in gratitude for all of the gifts I have received — for the reminder to breathe, to connect to my Beingness, and, most of all, to laugh and lighten up.

Universe, thank you, thank you, thank you.

Lilia Shoshanna Rae assists clients and students in their awakening process to connect more fully with the Divine and their soul purpose. Through individual intuitive healing sessions, meditations, and transformative teachings, such as the Enneagram, sacred geometry, and spiritual alchemy, Lilia guides her clients to their goals, one step at a time. Visit her website, www.LightLoveTruthWisdom.com/pebbles, where she blogs on topics of practical mysticism, and receive a free meditation on an MP3.

From Heartache to Heart Wide Awake

Linda Crawford

"NO, MOMMY, I DON'T WANT TO. Please, can we stay and live here like we used to?" the little voice echoed through my daughter's tears. I was standing in the living room feeling immense sadness as I looked around at blank walls and an empty house once filled with pictures, furniture, family, friends, and celebration. My younger daughter sat on the floor rather quietly as we held a ceremony honoring the sale of our home to say thank you for many memories. Witnessing this moment felt like someone had ripped my heart out, tossed it onto the floor, and then threw it back at my face for me to taste the bitter and painful experience of a broken marriage. This exact moment would be the experience that caused an intense trigger of unworthiness, guilt, and shame in the deepest places of my being.

That evening I stayed with my sister, as she insisted this would not be a time to be alone. As she and I lay in her bed, all I could do was cry.

I do not ever remember weeping with such intensity, and this type of burning I had never experienced before in my heart. It felt like someone had their hands squeezed around my neck, not leaving much room to breathe. My heart ached and I just wanted to crawl under a rock and die. The only position I felt I could be in for a little relief and comfort was the fetal position – the same position I was in before being born forty-one years ago. Perhaps I was giving birth to something not yet known and needed to be a little messy and uncomfortable first. I was grateful to be seen and heard in all of this, with my sister by my side, along with many other soul sisters and brothers, family, and friends. To this day I hold the deepest appreciation for their role in being a significant key to my well-being.

All I could think of in this intense moment of grieving, the last piece that held us together as "the family I knew," was all the mistakes I felt I had made. How I'd fallen short as a wife, as a mother to our children, and as myself. The trauma of the death of a relationship after two decades together, through dating and marriage, was intense. When tragedy strikes and leaves you standing naked for all to see your flaws, it forces you to look inside. I encourage you to go into this reflection when you have a nudge, as I assure you that this exploration will be one of the best choices you will ever make.

What was once a loving, committed, and connected relationship had grown filled with distance, frustration, and pain. And before I could fathom undoing the damage that I had caused on my end by being unconscious and not living the real dance of the feminine and masculine, I had to first recognize and acknowledge how badly disconnected our relationship had ended up. Communication, respect, and intimacy all fell short of both our expectations, and the process of forgiveness, acceptance, and understanding was the next essential journey.

The yearning and desire for something within myself was very strong — a longing for freedom the meaning of which I had still not really understood. I recognized I needed to make peace with the death of many aspects of our relationship as I knew it. Here is an excerpt from my journal — a practice I highly recommend during any transition:

> "In death, there is the release on every level of that which no longer serves us — of that which takes on new meaning, shape, and form before us — of that which opens up the birth of something else… so many unknowns. And to be at peace in the grieving of what is and was, that I may embrace fully, openly and without shame, new life, new creation in another manifestation of transformation. Death is inevitable in every way and I can learn to be with it, accept it, love it, and be set free."

I know that if you are reading this, you either know someone who is going through a transition, or you yourself are doing so, forcing you to look deeper at the important questions. For me it was "What about this situation is birthing the truth within me, awaiting to emerge, so that I may live free?" I believe with all my heart that crisis has the potential to be the catalyst for creating transformation that has been waiting to unfold, much like a caterpillar's potential to become a butterfly. Since I was very young, I have always been curious about the fields of human potential, psychology, the mystical, the spiritual, and everything in between, and have been judged at times for my incessant need to know, to grow, to evolve.

This is a part of me I have grown to love immensely, one of many I have made peace with as I accept that I am on an evolutionary path. Fundamentally, who I am is okay. Through your experiences of change and transition, the turn inward in preparation for what needs to be expressed in and through you is a critical piece of your birthright on this planet at this time. You are part of the web of the world, and invited to be the best version of you to support a new paradigm of an awakened humanity.

My voyage to greater peace, self-acceptance, and self-love from the dark shadows I was navigating was supported with an ongoing process of deep forgiveness of my husband and myself, knowing that we were innocently being and doing the best we knew how to in relation to our marriage. In fact, every step along the way was perfect, and not a defect. I could take the cross off my back, put the beating stick down, and embrace with grace where and who I am today as a result of the last four decades of my life. God does not create imperfection. My prayer was to awaken something beautiful seeking to emerge, to evolve beyond old patterns and thoughts, and to live with integrity. I wanted to experience joy and pleasure, ecstasy and vulnerability, and surrendered to God to support me.

Over time I had the capacity to open to receiving that which I yearned to know, understand, and create. Gratefully, it was a deepening of falling in love with me in a way I never had before. I freed myself from suffering and struggle, from the inside out, through powerful ways that I have the gift of teaching to others today. This path opened doors for me to attract more harmonious and conscious relationships. With a more compassionate and gentle heart, old hurts, pain, and aches began to melt, and being radically vulnerable was more the norm as I embraced my femininity, sexuality, and divinity. The expanding relationship to God became my devotion through prayer and gratitude.

As you walk this mystery of the unknown with faith, you will develop clarity about what is good about this time in your life. I discovered:

1. My husband and I created amazing memories and grew with each other to be where we are now, and co-created and

birthed two beautiful children to love unconditionally. We now have the opportunity to learn how to co-parent these precious angels consciously and respectfully.

2. This event in my life is what birthed my desire to support other women transitioning out of long-term relationships, to enhance and transform their lives through healing from the inside out, and to share the message of how to effortlessly dance with the masculine and understand and embrace the very nature of their instinctual being as well as our own with unconditional love and respect.

3. I am okay in my allegiance to the inner call for my own growth and my part in it on this sacred planet in preparation for our new Universal paradigm of greater peace, joy, love, and real heart-based connection to Oneness.

4. Freedom shows up through loving and accepting every choice, action, and decision I have made up to this point, knowing that Divine Perfection works through me. There is no blame... only enlightenment.

5. Expanding my awareness of the emasculation of men on our planet, owning my role in that, and making a pledge to no longer consciously participate in those ways gave me the op-portunity to celebrate and honor the masculine and heal my dysfunctional outlook regarding men and my inability to trust them.

6. The answer and solution is in ALL ways God.

Crisis, change, and transition unlock the door to feel the Beloved so your heart can open again to receive in its expansiveness. They re-veal the truth of the present moment, and that is love. Through all of the turmoil in the breakdown of our marriage, I knew that it was a time to see the blessings. This was an invitation for deeper honesty in owning the totality of myself, and therefore falling madly in love with all of it, with all of me. Remember, we are radiant, loving beings. Our light is never dimmed, no matter what pain and despair we are going through or experienced in the past. I invite you to remember the truth of who you are by asking, "What about this breakdown is good?" You will uncover the breakthrough, and in it your heart and soul will open wider awake.

"Take God's hand and walk your path in faith and grace." — Linda Crawford

Linda Crawford, the Transformational Goddess for single, separated, and divorced women, is on a mission to inspire 1 million women to heal all the relationships in their lives, especially the one with themselves, by becoming radically raw and honest. Through her private holistic practice, coaching, workshops, and books, Linda is a storyteller and vibrational healer, and she is in demand internationally for her wisdom and capacity to heal the soul. Sign up for her free ebook at www.TheLindaCrawford.com and begin creating magic.

Tribal Love

Louise Moriarty

WELCOME TO MY WORLD. I live in the land of the dreaming of an ancient culture of the earth. I acknowledge the lineage of all the ancestors who have walked before me, paving the way for us to have this experience. I also bless and acknowledge you for taking the journey of the truth seeker.

Lost Years

Something always felt like it was missing from my life. Sometimes I felt it was me, and sometimes my family, the system, or our culture. I wanted to be cradled in a certainty that I belonged and that people "got me."

To protect myself from the not happily ever after relationships I had thrown myself into, I shed my childhood skin and put on a tattoo amour to protect myself. This connected me to biker culture. Clustering together against the unfairness of the system and the authorities, we felt like our backs were covered.

Drugs were a big part of this way of life. Masking pain and grief became the priority. I became numb to how we were treating each other and alienating ourselves from what mattered to us. There were many times I wondered how I was going to survive.

I had run away from what was called normal into drug and love addiction, violent relationships, and blaming and fighting everyone and everything. I trashed and denied myself, shut down, and created suffering for myself and others around me. I tolerated all of it because I felt like I had a mob that would stick by me and let me express everything I felt, even the rage that had bubbled up inside me.

Eventually what I was running from was reflected more and more in the life I had created.

It was a neighbor who acknowledged my essence. She subtly intervened, without judgment. She gave me books of hope to read and saw through the "me" I had become, reinforcing the inner me that loved life and had a gift.

I started teaching and learning gymnastics again. I now had something to hold on to that I felt good about, that I was good at. I had re-learned the art of doing what I loved. This gave me a focus to walk away from the things in my life that weren't making me happy towards something that made me feel like the real me.

I was still looking for my tribe. I searched in one healing modality after another, exploring spiritual practices and studying social work. While on a placement interview, the woman asked me about my skills. I got excited about juggling, then dismissed it. She told me to never dismiss anything that made me smile like that, because you never know when it will come in handy.

I was starting to get my life back on track, filling up my tool kit with tricks and tips for healing, and wanted to start saving everyone with what had helped me.

New Circus Culture

I volunteered to teach gymnastics at a youth circus school. This gave me entrance into "new circus" culture. What I found was the first tribal culture that has grown to be global. No matter where I went, if I saw circus people, I could ask them where they were from and who they knew, and we would exchange skills and resources and start creating together. A big sense of family.

At student actions against uranium mining, some of us found out we were involved in community circus, and we had an instant connection. We could involve everyone in creating a show and get our message across in an entertaining and challenging way.

At that action, I was also blown away by the joy and natural agility of the Aboriginal kids in the desert. They had the aerial awareness to throw their bodies through the air. No technique, just the naturalness of a bird flying, and then always landing right side up like a cat. They were connected, and had no question that they belonged, even though it appeared that life had pulled the land out from under their feet.

My desire to steer teenagers and children away from the path on which I had gotten lost led me to American learning disabilities camps, an Indian orphanage, and then out to Far West New South Wales in Australia. Now circus was the vehicle. We could incorporate all the things I loved: circus, storytelling, dancing, poetry, music, and gardening, weaving them into programs, performances, and tours. Circus gave everyone a chance to explore their ability to create. We involved the whole community and linked to other communities around Australia that were also using circus with disaffected youth and adult survivors. We travelled to circus festivals where the young people were treated as equals with the professional circus artists.

Dreams Come True! Circus To Save the World.

What amazing dreams we made come true. People came from all over the world to share in this experience. The passion we had for what we were doing was like a magnet. We were blessed with support from Cirque du Monde, an offshoot of Cirque du Soleil, which supports circus programs for youth at risk in eighty countries around the world. We trained and collaborated with circus trainers and social workers from far and wide.

We found other people who were in agreement that circus could save the world. Reg Bolton, a legend who seeded much of the circus culture in Australia, had been "sprouting" this stuff for decades, his view being that circus is about knowing your strengths, showing off (being proud of who you are and your skills), taking risks, touching and trusting, knowing where you belong in the group, dreaming and aspiring, and having fun – all the basic needs of a healthy, developing being.

Now I give myself love and care as a first priority so I can have a full cup to give from. My passion will always be creating a love of life-long learning, through arts practices and celebrations, to enhance the world. I continue to share that vision of our evolutionary potential in my circus activities at events with communities, and woven into story-telling and multiple intelligence teaching in schools.

Being connected to circus people has reminded me to play and not take life too seriously. I found a tribe that I can run with.

It doesn't have to work that way just with circus people. The tribal skills uncovered in circus I now transfer to all my interactions, connecting to people from a heart space of what they love, giving my gifts, and supporting and serving them to enable their gifts to shine in these amazing times. We have never been so supported in our multiple tribal connections.

Taking responsibility for going towards what my heart truly loved to do changed everything. It began my return journey back out through hopelessness and despair.

Let the Impossible Become Possible for You

Still stuck? I dreamt that I could fly as a child. I still believe it's possible.

When I learned to tumble, I had the sensation of being able to trick the body into doing things that don't seem possible. I was flying. You don't have to somersault to get this awareness. Learning to juggle, or even mastering simple brain games, can create new connections between your right and left brain. Through these activities we grow the ability to link the creative and linear sides of our brains, enabling pathways of action towards our dreams.

Have an experience for yourself. Point one finger to your nose, then cross the other arm in front of your face to touch your ear, then swap them over. By practicing things that appear simple, you can learn that things aren't always as they seem. With practice, what seems impossible can become possible.

Connecting the right and left brain creates new pathways of movement in our bodies. Old habit patterns and emotions held in our bodies can create stress and disease. If we laugh out loud at our response, gain flexibility to attempt new activities, and get over our fears of failing and looking silly, we are rewiring everything.

Anytime we do things differently with our bodies, we are beginning to form new patterns of choice and action that enable us to explore new possibilities for ourselves.

So let yourself do something you have always wanted to.

For young people, or any one else looking to find their passions and a group that will nurture them, circus is a great starting place.

Now you have read something that I trust inspired you. Get out there and do more of the thing that makes your heart sing, and find the people who are singing in harmony with you. No matter how homeless, in debt, upset, or in regret you are, the place to start is to cheer yourself on and do one thing you love, for you. You'll find that the whole world can open up like... like a CIRCUS!

Louise Moriarty is passionate to restore the strengths of tribal culture on a global scale. She has a social work degree and a master's in social ecology. On her search for happiness, this free-spirited traveler gained skills in circus, clowning, and poetry. Utilizing spiritual and physical practices, she develops workshops and tools for community and personal evolution. See www.LouiseMoriarty.com for more tools for creating joy and a natural flow towards a love of life-long learning.

Embraced by the Wings of an Eagle

Lyn Abdullah

I HAVE ALWAYS BEEN FASCINATED BY EAGLES. If there is an animal I would want to be, it is undoubtedly an eagle. As a child I would often say, "An eagle is so fr–e–e!" So when I saw the title of Jeff Guidry's book, *An Eagle Named Freedom: My True Story of a Remarkable Friendship*, my eyebrows rose instinctively at seeing the words *eagle* and *freedom* together. My senses were fired up, and I found this story of a man's remarkable friendship with an eagle intoxicatingly intriguing. His story worked its way into my heart and triggered a transformation and a special awareness in me.

Jeff had the opportunity to nurse the injured Freedom back to health. Here are some of the most important lines from the book for me:

> "From the moment Jeff Guidry saw the emaciated baby eagle with broken wings, his life was changed. For weeks he and the staff at Sarvey Wildlife Care Center tended to the grievously injured

bird…Miraculously, she recovered, and Jeff, a center volunteer, became her devoted caretaker… [Years later] when he learned he was cancer free, Jeff's first stop was Sarvey to walk with Freedom. Somehow this special bird seemed to understand the significance of the day. For the very first time she wrapped both her wings around Jeff, enveloping him in an avian hug…"

"She wrapped both her wings around Jeff"… Wow! What an awesome feeling that must have been! What state of mind would you need to be in to be able to communicate at such a deep and meaningful level with an animal? What kind of unspoken message would you need to carry inside to cause an eagle to sense your thoughts and emotions with such acuity and demonstrate an un-canny, yet real sense of love for you – an avian hug! I equate such a state of mind with what I call an "Owner Mindset" – love-focused and inspired by gratitude and inner joy.

I have lived a journey of immense personal transformation, and I still love each new day of re-invention. In particular, I have become progressively aware of how I think and how I respond to life. This awareness influences the choices I make, resulting in a state of well-ness that enhances my vitality (especially increased energy levels), and helps me maintain a positive mental attitude. Often, this state trans-lates into awesome instances in which I find myself feeling happy for no reason! I like to call this "life gem" of mine "Effortless Daily Living."

Moving further, I would like to share with you the reasons why the Owner Mindset is a mantra for my "life gem," and the various punctuation points in my life that have reinforced the importance of taking ownership.

Ownership in our daily conscious living is the key to success with our goals and challenges. We demonstrate the Owner Mindset whenever we make a purpose-driven choice, and it is a powerful state of mind!

Achieving success is not rocket science; it is the result of taking full responsibility for how we choose to respond to any situation by asking, "What kind of person do I need to be to re-create or co-create a better situation, and what's my next course of action to make things happen?"

Every day, I do my level best to launch my own flights of personal freedom with choices that are based on my F-R-E-E-D-O-M manifesto:

Fly like an eagle
Rainy days happen
Enlist your subconscious mind
Engage your heart
Dive into things that light you up
On a clear day…
Mindset and **M**iracles

Fly Like an Eagle

Flying like an eagle means focusing on what's right with you – not on what's wrong with you – as you take yourself through life's journey. I can illustrate this focus by telling you about my transformational journey as a parent. Like most single moms, I face challenges in balancing a working life, parenthood, and running a household on my own. I live a major part of my day – every day – for my two boys in the midst of their teenage years, which is just as trying for me as it is for them. Focusing on what's right with me and my boys – my signature strengths as an individual and theirs – has helped me work through those dark days of inner struggle, frustration, and self-blame.

As a result, I have become more objective, and I am always "switched on" with an attitude that emphasizes "seeking first to understand" my children (as Steven Covey so rightly puts it) before stepping in with my authority as Mom. Nowadays, I feel that I am truly getting somewhere in my quest to be a "Super-Mom." I am still fine-tuning the formula, and I am excited about how far I have gone with this quest, thanks to flying like an eagle!

Rainy Days

Rainy days just happen sometimes. It took me a long time to realize that no matter how we fortify ourselves with the best attitude and the most positive thoughts, the rainy days of life do come pouring in when someone says the wrong thing at the wrong time, or when things don't go the way we planned.

When such things happen, I first ask myself, "Where is it written that I have to cry about this?" or "Where is it written that I have to be so upset?" Then I take ownership of my responses to such situations with these words: "When you fly in God's space and soar among the cotton-white clouds, there are bound to be rainy days, because those clouds do turn gray once in awhile so that rain can fall to enrich Mother Earth."

Enlist Your Subconscious

Enlist your Subconscious Mind, and keep close to God, for therein lie the solutions to your problems. Most of the problems I deal with involve relationships and how they impact my fervent desire to achieve my life goals. My Subconscious Mind needs only the goal of living my dream to work towards in order to reveal solutions for me.

Your mind is an amazing gift from God, and we have yet to under-stand fully how it works. But we can enlist our Subconscious to see problems as opportunities rather than showstoppers – opportunities to enhance personal empowerment.

Engage Your Heart

Engage your heart when it hurts most. I have learned through the wisdom of others that I am complete. When I involve myself in a ro-mantic relationship, it is because a soul mate could complement me, not complete me. It was a real effort to move from "Vulnerable Me" to "Just Me." I leaped across that chasm a few times without tasting success, and it caused a lot of pain in my heart. I allowed myself to see "Vulnerable Me" as incomplete, and hurt myself through my own lim-iting beliefs about relationships. Successfully being "Just Me" through engaging my heart has made an amazing contribution to my posture, and I am enjoying life so much more!

Dive In

Dive in to things that fire your passion and imagination, then dive deeper to reach your goal. In his book called *The Dip: A Little Book That Teaches You When To Quit (and When To Stick)*, Seth Goldman emphasizes, "When something (or someone, if I may add) is worth it, it is worth going through the Dip."

Seth calls these choice-related pathways "dips" in which we must decide to push ourselves towards our goals, or to get realistic and move away from situations or things that we don't love or want. He changed my thinking about how to run my business, and most im-portant, how to forge ahead every day towards progressive success milestones. When we "lean into the dip," we end up being more passionate and more creative in what we do, and the results can be pretty awesome!

On a Clear Day

"On a clear day you can see forever," as the saying goes; and it's true. Clarity paves the way for consciously and subconsciously working towards getting what you want. I learned a very effective goal-writing technique from a personal development program: Write your goals using positive words and phrases. Ensure that they do not include "low-vibration" emotions like "want" and "need." Rather, use words like "enjoying," "continuing," "loving," and "beginning." And remember that your goals are a process rather than an end result — a real winner for me!

Mindset and Miracles

Miracles and mindset go hand-in-hand. Experience is the best teacher, and the most painful experiences are often the ones that fortify us the most. These affirmations have helped me through tough times tremendously: "Fear and love cannot co-exist," "Love is a verb," "Love in the heart matters most," and "Love yourself first so that others can love the best of you." Love is the mindset that manifests the miracles we seek most in our daily lives — those that tug at our heartstrings and inspire us to move mountains and bear the most unbearable pain and sorrow, giving us hope for another wonderful tomorrow. Concentrate on the loving person you need to be to make things happen, and feel worthy of miracles coming your way.

So how was your day today? Did miracles bring a smile to your face and make you appreciate how wonderful this day has been, and how much more wonderful tomorrow will be because you lived today? Go ahead and manifest your Owner Mindset-driven results that are so important to effortless daily living – swooping, soaring, hovering, but never caged! Indeed, the power of courage, love, and a peaceful, relaxed mind allow you to take a daily flight with F-R-E-E-D-O-M!

Lyn Abdullah, a Professional Health Coach, certified Wellness Consultant and Nutrigenomics Practitioner, is passionate about helping people achieve success milestones in their transformational journeys towards long-term health and vitality. Lyn lives to inspire and be inspired by others. Continuously evolving and transforming, she looks forward to co-creating wonderful "life miracles" (big and small) with the people she connects with through her coaching and sharing sessions. To get her free ebook, *101 Ways to...*, visit www.HealthyCoachingWithLyn.com.

Becoming Your Own Soul Mate

Maeve Crawford

IMAGINE YOUR GREATEST PAIN becoming your greatest healing, your greatest challenge, your greatest teacher, and your greatest struggle that could heal the world.

My biggest struggle, which I thought I would never recover from, became the source of my greatest healing, and helped me realize my potential in this lifetime. I chose to take on the challenge, facing it head and heart on. I walked within, eventually discovering how to heal myself and then heal others. I never understood why I was here, yet I felt I was here for something other than work and washing dishes!

I married when I was in my twenties after falling madly in love with my husband. We'd decided to wait until we'd been married for a couple of years before we had a child, a son. Not realizing this marriage was temporary, when it came to an end I was devastated. I knew I had to get on with life as I now had a small child to look after alone. I hadn't a clue where to begin or how I would do this.

Soon after our divorce, my parents retired to the countryside, so I was now unable to drop by whenever things got really difficult. Time to grow up. This was one of those times when I wanted to crawl into a ball and hug my knees.

A few years later, after I had spent time on my own, I discovered I had a passion for supporting children with special educational needs. I then made a tough decision to leave my beloved role in a primary school to explore the world of university. It made no sense to many people in my life that at the same time I decided to begin a relationship with someone I barely knew. I'd been on my own for eight years, so I thought I'd done enough inner work to take everything on. Who knew what I was letting myself in for?

Two years after this relationship began, I was into my third year at university and now totally addicted to drugs and alcohol. The relationship came to an explosive and messy end, so my heart was once again in tatters. I lived in a worthless void where the drugs no longer provided an escape, and I realized that the person I thought loved me, didn't.

I'd lost myself completely in this relationship, and asked myself why I'd let this happen. I knew I wanted more for my life. I certainly wanted my son to grow up knowing what loving, healthy relationships looked and felt like. We had forged a great loving bond and I wanted him to feel less responsible for my happiness. He'd spend a great deal of time doing everything he could to make me laugh, even writing me letters to express his sorrow for my pain. What a beautiful child. He deserved more, and he became my inspiration, which spurred me to keep going when it seemed like there was nowhere to go.

I contemplated what love is all about and what it requires to have a satisfying love life. I realized I didn't know, so I embarked on a search to find out more about what makes relationships work and what prevented me from experiencing the love I so deeply desired. Little did I know that this quest would take me to the other side of the world!

I came across a relationship coach who instilled in me a confidence I hadn't felt before. He told me what I had never heard from a man, which made me wonder if it could be possible to hear this from the soul mate I might share my life with. What he really helped me understand was that what he told me, I ought to be able to tell myself... and believe!

I loved our calls, and always felt like another layer of myself had been peeled away, revealing an inner strength underneath. I often felt exposed and uncertain, fearful of what would come next. What he taught me often made me feel sad for what I hadn't learned before. My lesson caused such pain that I wanted to turn back the clock to relive what I'd experienced. Except this time I would do it all again differently, because I now felt empowered to make informed choices, and had become conscious that the power lay within me all the time.

I journaled daily and read books that helped me increase my self-confidence and awareness of who I am. Steadily I grew my level of self-worth and understood that the person I was meant to love is myself. This realization made me cry so much I thought I was going to flood the house! How could I love myself? I didn't know how. What did it mean to love myself?

So once more I embraced a new lesson to discover how to learn to love myself. I read books that taught me affirmations and the power of my thoughts. I read so many books, swimming in the words of healing, that these new tools carried me from a pit of despair to a place of hope and optimism.

I wrote affirmations on sticky notes and put them in places around the house. I even put some in my purse and took them out every now and then to remind myself of what I was aiming for. I'd look in the mirror, paying close attention to my thoughts on seeing my reflection. Instead of saying, "Oh my God, you fat, ugly thing!" I'd say lovely things, blow kisses to myself, and say, "I love you!" It became a fun experiment in learning to love myself, albeit tentative at first, and seemingly temporary.

I became skilled at learning to love myself, and by telling my reflection how much I loved myself, I started to believe it. One of the books I read encouraged me to fall in love with me. It made sense that if I wanted to fall in love with another, I really needed to fall in love with me first. Also, if I didn't love myself, I mean truly love myself, how could I ever expect anyone else to? I didn't know this before at the level I was beginning to understand it. I decided to take it a step further and make dates with myself. I went to the cinema, out for meals on my own, enjoyed long walks as though I were strolling along with the love of my life. Well, I really was, and the love of my life was ME!

Who knew?

I had so much fun with this that I thought I'd share it with one of my closest friends. She'd been with me through much of my breakdown, so I told her what I'd discovered. She thought it was fabulous. I arranged a night out with her and we went to one of our favorite places. During the day I decided to pamper myself in preparation for the evening. I went out shopping and bought a ring. I put it on as a symbol of my undying love for me.

When we went out that evening, my friend commented on the ring. I told her the reason behind my wearing it, which she thought was hilarious, and she didn't fully appreciate the significance of me marrying myself. I said that if I didn't want to marry myself or feel happy alone, then how could I ever expect to feel happy being with anyone else?

It wasn't long before I wrote my checklist for the type of life and relationship I desired. My life had undergone a huge transformation, and I now knew what it took to create the love life I had always wanted. My new affirmation became: "The person who comes into my life must love me more than I love myself!" I had come such a long way and knew there was not a chance that I was going back.

No longer settling, I made a commitment to myself that I'd rather stay on my own than be with someone for the sake of being in a relationship. What a huge turning point, as I'd previously felt honored if someone chose to be with me. I started to see myself as a "good catch" and felt certain about what I wanted for my life. What I'd learned and discovered, I felt compelled to share with as many people as possible. I didn't realize that this desire to share everything I'd learned would bring me closer to living my true life purpose and eventually connect me to my soul mate.

Maeve Crawford is a soul mate catalyst, love visionary, and relationship angel. Believing wholeheartedly in soul mates, she empowers conscious singles to transform their lives. Maeve is committed to ensuring that her clients achieve the results they desire. To work with Maeve, contact her at www.becomingyourownsoulmate.com. Be sure to download her free report, "How To Become Your Own Soul Mate," a ten-step guide to healing your heart and falling in love with YOU!

Access the Power of the Truth in You!

Marcelle Charrois

AS I DANGLE IN MID-AIR, I am terrified and in utter shock at how I got there! One minute I was playing with my friends at the camping playground, taking turns climbing the twenty-five foot ladder and sliding down the huge metal tube, and the next minute one of my friends had pushed me over the side, and as I watched in horror, started prying my fingers from the railing. My other two friends appeared at the top, and for a moment, I was relieved, thinking, "Surely they will pull me up!" One of the two grabbed my right arm, and to my surprise, held it limply as the other just stood there watching and the third continued to peel my fingers off the railing... one... by one... by one. My body hit the hard-packed sand below, and my breathing was abruptly halted. In excruciating pain, I concluded, "I am going to die!"

Maybe I should not have told them about my secret. Up until then, it had struck a funny bone with most people when I would announce,

"Well, you must understand. I am from Mars. That's where my name comes from." So what had changed? When I first started school, kids often mocked, "Marcelle? That's a boy's name!" One day I triumphantly neutralized the barbs with my brilliant idea of announcing my extraterrestrial identity.

However, on that fateful day, I really started believing that I must be from another planet. Betrayed by those I thought were my best friends, my seven-year-old sense of worth, security, and belonging was shattered. Consequently, fear and mistrust started to creep in. I began to see the world as a dangerous place, and that the only way to be safe was to trust no one and be self-sufficient and invisible.

Ever feel like you have been made captive in the "box of acceptability," adrift in a sea of social standards, perceived limitations, debilitating beliefs, and labels about what life should and should not be?

If so, rest assured. All is not lost! You are gifted with a personally calibrated tool that has always been inside of you. It is "Your Truth Navigator," and it has everything you need to direct and shift the tides in your life! Here is what it will do for you:

- Reconnect you with the strength and power of your intuitive heart
- Rebuild the bridge to your innermost longings and desires
- Serve as your most effective compass in achieving your goals
- Help you make decisions that are in alignment with your purpose
- Reset you onto your true self's authentic path

I got a glimpse of the power of this innate tool when I first told my peers of my alien origins. Without realizing it, I had harnessed the pure magic of shifting to my truth. If I could go back in time and share one thing with my childhood Martian self — a persona that embodied the essence of my unique inner truth — it would be the following: "The best life you can create for yourself is one that intimately knows, expresses, and honors YOUR truth!"

It is a simple, yet powerful message that could have diminished the effects of so many experiences that, over the years, ate away at me and had me shrink and bury piece by piece of myself deep down inside my being. I could have altogether staved off the 2008 health collapse that forced me to leave my work, barely able to function, and with no savings to fall back on.

Although I would have preferred to avoid all that pain and suffering, today I am very grateful for the illness that allowed me to break free from the stupor that had me so disconnected from my authentic self. After three years of journaling, writing, counseling, and health recovery-focused efforts, I proudly took back my identity… and I am here now, sharing my journey with you as well as the process that allowed me to reclaim my life!

People and events in the "outside" world will keep raising their *"reality flags"* at you about what *you, and only* you are qualified to know as the unique truth about who you are and what you can or cannot do or accomplish.

The good news is that there is a way to completely redefine your life – a way to reconnect with the irrefutable truth that shouts out: **"You are beautiful just as you are, and your truth is the only truth that matters!"** Your specific makeup and experiences have shaped you into the person that you are meant to be and continue to become. In fact, every challenge is an invitation to see the bigger picture and honor the truth within you.

Whenever the outside world comes knocking with its "That's life" rhetoric, it is your cue to engage **Your Truth Navigator** by using a thought, feeling, action, and result shifting process that I refer to as **"Stop, Reverse, and Celebrate!" (SRC)**. Let us now explore the steps with an example that will serve as a blueprint for living your heart's true desires:

Valerie has been in the corporate world for fifteen years and has always dreamed of starting her own business in fashion consulting. She has been talking about her long-held aspiration with work colleagues. Each time she is met with various reasons why it would not work or be too risky to even try. Determined to fulfill her dream, Valerie decides to use the SRC process to shift and reconnect with her truth.

1. Stop (S) – First, sit quietly, take slow and deliberate deep breaths, tune in to your heartbeat, and connect to your feelings about what occurred in the situation at hand. Acknowledge and take note of your feelings, and identify who or what caused those feelings to surface, as well as whether or not this is about you.

Valerie:

"What am I feeling? *Fear, uncertainty, discouraged, deflated.*"

"What/who caused me to feel this way? *My colleagues' feedback.*"

"Is this really about me? *No, it is other people's perceptions.*"

2. Reverse (R) – Then, engage your thought process to unveil your individual truth. This is when you can actually move through the feelings by activating Your Truth Navigator. What you will often discover here is that "your truth" is the reverse of the initially triggered thoughts and feelings.

Valerie:

• "What do I choose to believe about myself? *I know that I can do it because I am determined, passionate, resourceful, and have the vision, skills, and knowledge!"*

- "What do I wish to create in my life starting now? *My own business and the life that I truly desire.*"

- "What can I think, feel, and do differently to produce the results I wish to achieve? *I can choose to focus on my abilities and strengths; be grateful for my current employment which allows me financial stability while I work on establishing my business; research other successful fashion consultants, model their journey and best practices, and attend trade events.*"

- "What learning can I draw from this? *My dreams are mine to own, define, shape, and implement!*"

- "What am I grateful for? *I have the ability to create my life and choose my direction, and the love and support of my family and friends.*"

3. Celebrate (C) – Finally, now that you have revealed your truth and the right path for you, deliberately engage in active validation and celebration of this truth! To do so, determine which concrete actions you will take to accomplish your highest ideals, and the most joyful living experience of your goals and dreams. Last, but not least, create within yourself as much positive energy and excitement as you can to boost the manifestation power of your actions!

Valerie:

- "How can I validate, reinforce, and celebrate with concrete actions the truth that has just been revealed? *I will develop and implement a detailed business plan which will include a trip to the top fashion event in the world.*"

- "How can I maintain and amplify my enthusiasm and motivation? *Create a photo collage or video of my goals and look at it every day; visualize lucrative consulting contracts and picture myself already doing the work!*"

Just imagine what Valerie will have created in her life a year from now! Think about how you can apply this in your life and what it could mean for you, your family, and your community.

There is an unlimited intuitive power within each and every one of us. With its finely tuned compass, **Your Truth Navigator** faithfully puts you at the helm as the true captain of your life. It is up to you to consistently connect with, tap into, and act upon its unwavering wisdom.

Your true destiny awaits you with the richness and fullness of all the colors of the rainbow. Believe it, commit to it, and take purposeful and uplifted action by integrating **SRC** shifting into your daily reality. Step into it with both feet and experience the purest and highest form of freedom available to you – the freedom of your soul!

As a heart intelligence coach, Marcelle Charrois draws upon her wide-ranging background and experience with yoga, meditation, metaphysics, and natural healing to help people create their best life today! Her first book, *The Alien in Your Closet,* empowers you to reconnect with your intuitive instincts, true identity, and passion, while actively reversing the illusions of social conditioning. For access to her books, including her evolving children's series, programs, and complimentary tools and resources, visit her community at www.True2HeartLiving.com.

The Magic of Letting Go: Intention, Attention, No Tension

Marci Shimoff

FOR THE FIRST THIRTY-SIX YEARS of my life, I had been very achievement-driven. I worked hard, pushed myself, and was crystal clear about what I wanted. But I wasn't very good at letting go, relaxing, and opening to receive what the Universe brought me.

Early in my career, I'd learned a wonderful formula for manifesting anything in life from Bill Levacy, one of my life coaches. The formula consists of three rhyming steps:

- **Intention:** Be very clear about what you want.
- **Attention:** Focus your attention on what you desire. Make sure your thoughts, words, feelings, and your actions are in alignment with your intention.
- **No tension:** Relax, let go, be in a state of ease, and open to receive from the Universe.

While I was really good at those first two steps — intention and attention — I had a hard time with the "no tension" step, even though the most wonderful miracles have come to me when I've been able to let go into "no tension." Perhaps the most dramatic example of this relates to my biggest career breakthrough. Let me share the story with you.

I was thirteen when I attended my first event featuring an inspirational speaker, Zig Ziglar. As I saw him walking the stage, passionately giving his speech and moving the entire audience, I said to myself, "That's what I'm supposed to do here on this planet." I had a very clear intention and vision. I saw myself traveling around the world inspiring millions of people to live their best lives possible. At that young age, my **intention** was clearly set.

My attention was also strong. For years, I did everything I could to support that intention happening. Eventually I got an MBA in Training and Development (the closest degree I could find to match my intention), started my career as a corporate training consultant, and taught seminars on stress management and communication skills in Fortune 500 companies across the United States. I read every self-help book I found, attended every self-help seminar I could, studied other speakers' delivery styles, learned every self-development technique out there, and followed the success principles I'd discovered in order to make my dream a reality.

I was fortunate to have an amazing mentor in Jack Canfield — years before the *Chicken Soup for the Soul* books had even been conceived. He taught me (and many others) how to deliver self-esteem training programs. Soon after I attended his "Train the Trainer" course, I began teaching those programs to women. Though I was having some success working for a seminar company teaching one-day training programs, I was frustrated because I wasn't having the big success I'd dreamed of.

On top of that, I was exhausted. I felt like a road warrior, traveling 200 days a year. I would speak all day long (in high heels), then get in a car at 5:30 pm and drive three to four hours to the next city, fall fast asleep, and wake up early the next morning so I could be in the training room by 7:00 am, ready to do that routine all over again. I did that day in and day out.

And while I knew in my heart that inspiring people was what I was supposed to be doing, I sensed that there was something bigger that was supposed to happen. My vision was to reach more people worldwide, but I couldn't seem to break through to the next level in my career. I'd hit a wall.

Tired, confused, and drained, I started doubting my future: *What was next and how could I get there?*

As grace would have it, my dear friend, Janet Atwood, took me by the hand one day and said, "Marci, you're coming with me. You're burned out. You need a break. We're going on a seven-day silent meditation retreat." Shocked, I answered, "No way. I haven't been silent for more than two hours in my life! I can't imagine seven days of silence. Impossible." But Janet was insistent, so off we went to a week of what I thought would be silent torture.

The first few days were really challenging, but I finally settled in to the silence and started enjoying the ease that came with it. On the fourth day, in the middle of a meditation, a light bulb went off in my head, and I saw the words *Chicken Soup for the Woman's Soul*. As soon as I had that vision, I knew exactly what I was to do next – write that book.

At the time, only the original *Chicken Soup for the Soul* book had been published, and nobody had thought of creating other specialty books. I just knew this was it – something that would touch many people and that was a calling for me! This was, I felt, a gift from the Universe.

The only problem with the scenario was that I still had three more days of my silent retreat left. I'd just had the great epiphany of my life and I couldn't tell anybody!

As soon as the silence was over, I ran to the closest pay phone, called up Jack, and said, "Listen to this: *Chicken Soup for the Woman's Soul.*" He said, "What a great idea! I can't believe nobody's thought of this before." He then called his publisher and said, "*Chicken Soup for the Woman's Soul,*" to which the publisher replied, "What a great idea. I can't believe nobody's thought of this before."

Within a few months I had a signed contract to co-author the book with Jack, Mark Victor Hansen, and my business partner, Jennifer Hawthorne. A year and a half later, *Chicken Soup for the Woman's Soul* was released, and in its first week it hit #1 on the *New York Times* bestseller list. Since then, I've written a total of nine books that have sold fifteen million copies in thirty-three languages, and I've travelled around the world speaking about the messages in those books.

Relaxing into a deep state inside – the state of **no tension** – is what led to that pivotal "A-ha!" moment that transformed my career. It was proof to me that it's those three steps – intention, attention, and no tension, *together* – that create magic in our lives.

Working on *Chicken Soup for the Woman's Soul* was more fulfilling than anything I'd ever done before in my career, as it was birthed out of pure inspiration. I could feel that I was moving in tune with the Universe – that I had plugged in to something bigger than me; I had just gotten on the train, and it was moving me forward.

After the book came out, I was quickly speaking to audiences 100 times bigger than those I was used to speaking to – I was reaching 10,000 people instead of 100 people at an event. And the best part was feeling like I was fulfilling my life purpose.

As time went on, I met amazing teachers who had been my

idols in the transformational field. They were becoming my colleagues and friends, and I felt more empowered and more deeply fulfilled. I was getting to play in a bigger way.

Life After *Chicken Soup*

After I finished my seventh *Chicken Soup* book in seven years, I knew it was time to move on. I was burned out again. I was full of Chicken Soup. I'd lost the excitement and joy, and I sensed there was something else ahead for me. Remembering the magic formula, I decided it was time for another relaxation, ease cycle. I felt a pull toward deep inner reflection.

I believe we each have cycles in life — very active, outward cycles and then quieter, inward times. I had just completed an extremely active cycle, and I was craving some time to relax and go inside.

It wasn't easy for me to honor that desire to take it easy. Growing up, I always felt I had to stay busy, to be in constant motion. And certainly that feeling was reinforced by living in a society that focuses heavily on the outer cycle and doesn't tend to respect the power of the inner cycle.

But I'd gotten such a major lesson in the power of relaxing that whenever I felt guilty about taking some time off, I quickly remembered the good that came out of it.

So I took time off and did some soul searching: *What did I want to do next in my career?* I realized that I wanted to focus on happiness — researching the subject and finding out how people could experience greater happiness from the inside out. This was something I wanted, and that I wanted to be able to share it with others. (As the old saying goes, we teach what we most want to learn.)

After beginning the book, I went away on another silent meditation retreat to come up with the book title — this time I decided on a four-day retreat. (I figured that my *Chicken Soup* epiphany had come on the fourth day of my earlier week-long retreat, so I'd be efficient and give this one just four days.)

During the first three days of the retreat, while I wrote down more than 200 title ideas, none of them really excited me. But sure enough, during my meditation on the fourth morning, the title *Happy for No Reason* came to me, and I knew that was the next book. It described exactly the type of happiness that I was exploring and writing about. Once again, I felt the Universe had delivered a beautiful gift.

That book was truly a work of my heart. I learned so much in the process of writing the book — and I became much happier by applying what I learned. It worked.

Once *Happy for No Reason* was out in the world, I did some more soul-searching, and it became clear to me that the next book I wanted to write was about unconditional love, the kind of love that doesn't depend on a person, situation, or romantic partner — the love that is our essence. That's how my ninth book, *Love for No Reason*, was born. It feels as though this book, too, had been conceived from inspiration.

I'm thrilled that both of these books also became *New York Times* bestsellers, and that their messages of unconditional love and happiness have reached many people around the world. This is further proof that when I relax and let the Universe flow through me, the benefits are infinitely more profound.

Tips for No Tension

These days, whenever I feel out of balance or stuck, I lean into that "no tension" step of my magic formula. That's what puts me back into the flow of creativity and love.

Since the art of letting go is still something I haven't mastered, I think of three words that help remind me how to relax into no tension. Perhaps they'll help you:

The first word is "trust." Trust yourself and trust life. Ask, *"What can I do to move into that state of ease? What's the next step for me? What expands me?"* Then trust your inner voice to move in that direction.

The second word is "courage." Have the courage to hang in there, get through the difficult times, and keep moving forward. No matter what it looks like on the outside, listen to your heart and have the courage to follow it.

The third word is "compassion." We need compassion, particularly with ourselves. Remember, in the midst of whatever challenge you may be facing, offer yourself care and understanding. Nurture and nourish yourself. You'll be able to get through anything if you can be gentle, loving, and compassionate with yourself.

People often ask me if taking care of themselves and focusing on their own inner happiness and love is selfish. Absolutely not. On the contrary, I believe it's the least selfish thing that you can do. The more fulfilled you are, the more you're able to offer to the world. The world gets the benefit of your elevated energy. That concept is reflected beautifully in my favorite Chinese proverb:

When there is light in the soul, there will be beauty in the person.
When there is beauty in the person, there will be harmony in the house.
When there is harmony in the house, there will be order in the nation.
And when there is order in the nation, there will be peace in the world.

My wish you for you is that you feel the love in your heart and the light in your soul. May we each experience that love and light so we can light up and transform this world.

Marci Shimoff is a #1 *New York Times* bestselling author, a world-renowned transformational teacher, and an expert on happiness, success, and unconditional love. Marci's books include the *New York Times* bestsellers *Love for No Reason, Happy for No Reason,* and six titles in the phenomenally successful *Chicken Soup for the Woman's Soul* series. Her books have sold more than fifteen million copies worldwide in thirty-three languages. Marci is also a featured teacher in the international film and book sensation, *The Secret.* Visit her website at www.Happy-ForNoReason.com.

Death and Beyond
– Heaven on Earth

Rev. Marilee Ann Snyder–Nieciak, BSc

ACCORDING TO MERLIN, "A wizard is someone who lives their life backwards." I am a wizard. I died at twenty-six, became an entrepreneur at thirty-six, discovered spirituality and shamanism at forty-six, married at fifty-six, and became an author at sixty-five.

On December 12th, 1972, I was working for the Australian Consulate in Chicago. I was in my office, coughing, when co-workers said I really needed to go to the hospital. So off I went to the emergency room.

In the ER, I was told that my right lung had collapsed from a body full of blood clots. I was NOT going anywhere except to a hospital room, then to the nuclear lab. I was sitting on the side of the bed, smoking a cigarette, totally unaware of how "sick" I was, when they brought oxygen for me.

No one honestly believed my survival was possible. The doctor said, "You will die. All we can do is give you oxygen and blood thinners every four hours to dissolve the blood clots. But if you survive, you can never have children, and you need to lose fifty pounds and quit smoking." I told him no one was knocking at my door.

The next thing I knew, I was in the upper corner of my room looking down at my body lying in bed. Everything was grey – my body, the sheets, the walls, and the floor. Then there was THE LIGHT.

The air was different; it shimmered and sparkled, full of crystal particles. It was soft, like mother of pearl – shimmering very pale colors of pink, lavender, turquoise, yellow-gold, and silver-white – nothing I have ever experienced on Earth. I can go there any time, as if it just happened.

Lush, green, rolling hills climbed gently towards a low line of purple mountains. Behind the mountains was the most extraordinarily bright, luminous Light of gold and white, very different from the air. It was "The Other Side." I heard an almost inaudible singing, and felt soothed, caressed, and nurtured.

Faces with no bodies greet me. I know them – my great-grandparents and my granddaddy. The Other Side feels very safe and loving. For the first time I can remember, I have no physical, mental, emotional, or spiritual pain. There is just the most incredible sense of peace, unconditional love, and compassion for myself, everyone, and everything.

Feeling safe allowed me to hear my family say, "The choice to stay and never feel pain again is yours." For up to that moment, my life had been filled with fear and pain from orthopedic surgeries, continual psychic attacks, and the emotional and benign neglect of my mother. I had taken on her fears, trying to make everything "okay" to make her like me.

Then there was my brother's alcoholic abuse, which escalated upon his return from two tours in Viet Nam. My mother never acknowledged his addiction. During this same time, at twenty-three, I was raped at gunpoint after moving to Chicago's Near North. I came home only to be sent to my room. Mom never once discussed the incident. I had a figure like Sophia Loren, yet Mom continually gave me mixed messages, saying that I was fat, ugly, yet extremely intelligent. It wasn't fun being me.

As I stared at this incredible, bright, loving Light, my life flashed before me. For the first time I knew that "God" existed, and is loving, kind, and compassionate – huge revelation for an agnostic.

In an instant there was a knowing. I remember saying to my grandparents, "I have to go back. There is something that I have to do." No specifics, just that I was to go back. I woke up in the most excruciating pain, like I was being stabbed in the back on my right side. For the fifth time in twenty-six years, I was hospitalized.

What I remember the most from my death experience was this incredible gift of LOVE – actually experiencing it for the first time. It has been a long, continual journey, through each decade from the beginning until now, of transformation and remembering who I really am.

Grace and faith came to me with the shifting from linear to circular thinking, trusting my knowing. Having learned this as a small child full of light, I did know the Truth. I remember saying to my friends, "My heart is so full of love, and I don't know what to do with it."

"Your vision will become clear only when you can look into your own heart. Who looks outside, dreams; who looks inside, awakens."
– Carl Jung

Our vision is a reality – Heaven on Earth. I live on twenty-one acres of woodland called Sage Spirit Terra, meaning "Healing Spirit Land." It is a long way from Chicago, and many years in the making, for first it was a vision that started long ago in the dreamtime.

Yet in 1963, everything had changed. I'd won every award available in my first year of Junior Achievement, and attended their national convention. Then my Dad told me that the family was moving to Chicago, and they would leave me behind in Indiana with my grandparents to finish high school. Everyone moved in August. In September my Granddaddy died, leaving me with my grieving Grandmother.

In 1965, I needed my father's written permission to attend Purdue University's Krannert School of Business. Paying for my own education, I graduated in 1969, one of only five women who graduated that year.

After healing from the blood clots and receiving emotional counseling, one day in 1974 I quit my job and booked a flight to Italy. Thanks to a pickpocket in Milan, I lived creatively on $400.00 and my rail pass for six weeks. I started to awaken.

Upon returning, friends put me to work renting subsidized housing in a Chicago ghetto, which led to a successful national career in real estate nationwide. Dale Carnegie classes in 1976 helped me with self-esteem, but I still did not know or love myself.

In 1982, I met Sonia Choquette, who gave me a reading and said, "Marilee, you need to make the inside as beautiful as the outside." What I have since learned is that transformational healing comes from the inside out, from above down, on the whisperings of Spirit.

In 1982, I attended a Landmark Education weekend. I founded my first business marketing and managing high-rise buildings in Chicago. In 1988, I opened Gold Coast Cleaning & Contracting. This gave me weekends and evenings off to study in my sacred, secret garden. After fourteen years, I gave the business to my employees.

Rumi said, "Your task is not to seek for love, but merely to seek and find all the barriers within yourself that you have built against it."

From 1991 until now, my healing and growth has been exponential. Linda Howe taught me the Akashic Records. Michael Harner and Sandra Ingerman are my Shamanic teachers for journeying, extraction, divination, Soul Retrieval, and carrying Souls home. Michael Soto is Reiki Master to Anthony Pizzoferrato, my Reiki Master. Each provided spiritual awakening with direct revelation, insights, experiential and transformational healings, and many initiations.

Indigenous teachers started coming into my life in 2000. Ipupiara and Cleicha came to my "Healing Waters" event on the crystalline sands of Lake Michigan in 2001 and 2002, which we continued with our store, Earth Partners, a spiritual store where we met the Mitchel-Hedges crystal skull. I learned quantum healing with Young Living Essential Oils, and with extensive training I became internationally certified in Quantum Biofeedback. In 2005, I was initiated as a Purification Lodge Keeper and Pipe Carrier. Each modality is quantum healing, because it is from Source/God, Creator.

In 2007, using everything I know plus forgiveness of myself, I transmuted the cancer in my liver, right lung, and breast as my deceased sister stood guard. When the forgiveness was complete, she left, covering me with a blanket of light. I was then awarded a Sundance Buffalo Skull in May, and hosted the "World Drum" in July at Sage Spirit Terra.

During these years I cried buckets of tears as I experienced many setbacks, deaths, and bankruptcy. With continual meditation, prayer, forgiveness, and ceremony, my consciousness expanded to include, to accept, and to embrace both the light and the darkness, including those souls who lower their light to teach.

In dying, the Shaman is shown the Oneness of the web of life. I experienced "The Light" as the light of individual souls, like the individual leaves on the black tree branches of the "One Tree." By definition, I am "Wounded Healer/Shaman," learning to heal myself to help others.

In 2011, I was given a new assignment. "Write about the original thirteen crystal skulls." To write, once a month, for six months, I needed soul retrievals to remove the fear, doubt, and pain, and to receive love, confidence, and trust.

Shifting into my heart, I continually heal my barriers to love, raising my vibration and consciousness, thus allowing space for you to make the paradigm shift to be kinder and more loving. I came back to love you as your shaman, healer, and teacher.

What will you do?

Reverend Marilee Ann Snyder-Nieciak, BSc, is a Transformational Shaman, Healer, Author, and has been an entrepreneur since 1982, learning about therapeutic essential oils and ancient healing arts in Chicago. She opened Sage Spirit Terra in 1996. Rev. Marilee is a Reiki Master/Teacher, Akashic Records Teacher and Certified Shamanic Practitioner specializing in Drum Circles and Soul Retrieval. In 2004 she was consecrated a Bishop for Teaching and Spiritual Awakening. To learn more, visit Marilee at http://www.SageSpiritTerra.org. For your FREE gifts, visit http://bit.ly/marileesnydergift.

Heart Choice

Mary Dirksen

MY WORST NIGHTMARE VISITED ME the afternoon I received a certified letter in the mail. The document was one page, stating that my children desired to take up residency at their father's address. My daughter had just reached her thirteenth birthday that very weekend. My son would be fifteen in another four weeks, both of legal age to choose which parent to live with.

I looked at their signatures for long moments, attempting to find some sign of forgery or forced handwriting. I knew they couldn't possibly have signed the petition on their own. They must have been threatened, or worse, bribed.

But they were not with me. Their father refused to bring them home the night before, telling me they didn't want to go home and they didn't need to speak to me. After that short phone conversation with him, I braced myself for another battle in court. It seemed I had been in court regularly over the previous two years since our divorce had been finalized. It was a long, strenuous night for me. Fear gnawed at my stomach throughout my restless sleep.

My pain was unfathomable. I felt crushed and defeated. I was afraid, ashamed, and humiliated. I felt guilty. I combed my memory looking for all that I did so wrong to make them want to leave. I was angry and blamed others. For weeks I was tortured with scenes of slow, brutal deaths by my hands of my ex-husband, his wife, and his mother – the culprits who convinced my children to leave my home. In my thoughts I blamed my family and friends for not helping me talk to the kids about staying with me. I felt helpless and alone. At times I wanted to die. I wondered what others would think of me, because, after all, children don't leave their mother unless she's a very bad one.

Six weeks went by before I had to appear in court with my former husband to hear the amended custody arrangement and the granting of my visitation schedule. That also turned out to be the first time I had seen my kids since the weekend they left for their dad's and didn't come back. No words were spoken as they stood next to their stepmother, yet our eyes met momentarily from across the hall. I thought a bullet had pierced my heart. Why did their stepmother come? It was none of HER business, and certainly the kids didn't need to be put through any of this! How could she and my ex-husband be so inconsiderate of the kids?

I had written a lengthy letter to my children. I am sure God helped me write it because I was inspired by words that would take away any guilt from them in making an adult decision in the situation of having to choose between parents. I wanted them to know how much I missed them, but not to be concerned about me because I would be fine, and I really did understand their needing time with their dad, too. I saved it for their first visitation with me, and gave it to them to take home and read in private.

The letter was also therapeutic for me. I really had to trust God now – that He would take care of them and send them back to me when they needed me. I trusted Him to allow them to get what they went to their father's home for, and I prayed for peace in their hearts and minds. In turn, I started to have a little peace in mine. I began to pray, and meant it, something I hadn't done since before high school. I didn't believe in God, but I NEEDED Him.

Visitations granted me an appreciation for my time with my children, something I had taken for granted before. I recalled all the times when I had complained to myself about how overwhelmed I was with the responsibilities of being a mother. Before the divorce, I felt like I had the entire world on my shoulders. I was not only taking care of my children, but also my husband, our home, our bills, my job, and on and on. Afterwards, as a single mother, I didn't have money or time to do things with the kids. All of a sudden I had both, and my weekends with my children were completely focused on them. We started bonding.

As time passed, my anger eased. I found ways to bury some of my strong emotions, much like I did in childhood and in my marriage, with periodic outbursts from time to time over petty issues just to release my stress. I became a workaholic. I enrolled in college. I became obsessed with my plants and animals. In the meantime, my children grew, as did our relationship with each other. We took nothing about our family for granted.

By the time I earned my bachelor's degree, my children were grown, and each had a child of their own. I no longer needed my job to support them, and began thinking more about myself, something that was very strange for me, since I was always taking care of everyone else's needs first. I had been programmed since childhood to think of others first, otherwise I was being selfish and self-absorbed. And that was sinful, but now it was my turn to truly live. So I quit my job and a year later I moved across the country to Florida, 1000 miles away from all my family and friends.

The entire time I lived in Florida I felt as though a Guardian Angel was watching over me. One thing after another challenged me, yet there was always a savior nearby. When I was involved in an accident that rendered my car inoperative, a person I had recently met offered to let me stay with her so she could take me to work the following days. Another person I had just met loaned me his car a few days later to use until mine was out of the garage. Countless other people were there for me as I found myself stranded in helpless situations.

It was through one of my new friends in Florida that I started attending a church which was very different from that of my Catholic upbringing. One of the prayers that baffled me more than any other had to do with being thankful for our pain. I had had so much! It was several years before I understood that prayer. That was the beginning of my change in thought and change in attitude.

After three years in Florida, circumstances arose that forced me to return home. I was broke and had to take an hourly position until I could decide on my next move forward in life. I found myself paying more attention to all the apparent "coincidences" that had taken place in my life, and understood that they were nothing short of miracles. And they continued.

My new job provided an opportunity to go back to school as well as a number of other offerings. I was restless, and became an active participant in a number of groups within my company, the school I attended, and the community where I resided. My network expanded quickly.

After acquiring my MBA, attaining a few promotions, holding officer positions in several organizations, completing many hours of volunteer work in the community, and participating in extra-curricular activities at work such as serving on teaching and safety committees, I was still unfulfilled. I knew there had to be more for me in this life. I continued studying and reading, and attended workshops, retreats, and classes. I was becoming more and more spiritual, taking the discovery of myself and truth to a higher level. I was beginning to put together everything that had happened in my life as though it were a puzzle and each event was a piece of it. I was remembering the pain of the greatest challenges, and the circumstances of my darkest intervals, and how they pushed me forward into going back to school, building my finances, and strengthening me. I considered the miracles, such as my close relationships with my children and grandchildren in spite of geographical distance, my move out of state, and learning to venture alone, complete with an awareness of a divine presence with me always.

I was in a predicament. I was discontented with my job, yet I was earning more money than in any job I had previously held. I felt trapped. I reflected on my journey of heartbreak and blessings, and saw the path where it was leading. I was destined to make a difference in this world. I began to think about my options. Was I going to follow my heart and make my life happen, or continue as a victim and wait for life to happen to me?

In my mind I heard Wayne Dyer's words: "Let go and let God." With a deep breath I chose to trust my heart and listen to what I "felt" God was telling me. I hired a business coach and found my purpose using my skills, education, and, most of all, the knowledge I had gained from my pain. I left my hourly job and became an entrepreneur, serving as a Life Coach for mothers who have lost custody of their children. I intend to be their voice.

After retiring from corporate America, Mary Dirksen dedicated herself to becoming an entrepreneur and Life Coach to women who have lost custody of their children. With over twenty years of experience in dealing with trauma, she is one of the leading coaches in transforming pain to pleasure in women's lives. Grab a copy of her free ebook, *8 Critical Steps To Transforming Your Life after Losing Custody!* at www.MaryDirksen.com.

From Fear to Courageousness: The Power of Story

Mehrish Khan

IS THERE ANY PERSON ON THE PLANET who doesn't wish they had a manual for life? I seriously doubt it.

I don't know what you've been through so far in your journey, but because you're reading this, I would guess that something has triggered inside you a desire to seek some answers to your questions.

I may be relatively young on the outside, but I feel a lot older inside. My life has been a massive collection of hurtling obstacles. My own fears and insecurities have made me feel as if I were being buffeted by the menacing, crashing waves of an unforgiving sea, where life happens to you and you are a helpless passenger or a victim.

But then on the other side, there have been times of utter peace and serenity, when everything in my life just flowed, when with effortless ease everything clicked, and I felt somehow "whole." You know what I'm talking about, right?

It is the duality of being a victim, like a passenger out of control on a roller coaster ride, while at the same time finding glimpses of tranquility and paradise that led me deeper inside. That triggered me to ask questions: "Is this how it's supposed to be? Do I have the power to control and influence how my life turns out, or am I stuck on this roller coaster ride forever? Am I really a victim or do I have the power to change my story?"

It all started for me when I experienced a massive upheaval as a ten-year-old and left my roots in Germany, leaving the only life, friends, lifestyle, culture, and environment I had ever known. At such a young age, I was not aware of what moving from a small town to a city like New York entailed. Any childish excitement I felt at the prospect of such a move disappeared when I found myself sitting in a classroom in an American school, listening to all the incomprehensible words coming out of the teacher's mouth in a language I couldn't even understand, let alone speak. It was no surprise when I failed test after test for an entire year.

Gradually my family and I began to adapt to the American lifestyle. All seemed to be going well until one night when four masked and armed men broke into our family home and held us at gunpoint while they ransacked the house for anything of value. "This is our home," I remember thinking. "This isn't supposed to happen to us. We're supposed to be safe and secure here!" I was huddled up on the bed, shivering in fear, able to feel my sister's thumping heart as she lay next to me in the darkness. All I could think was, "Are they going to kill us?"

The feelings of victimization and lack of control did not stop there. Before I knew it, we were yet again moving, as the events of September 11th, 2001, swiftly concluded our stay in America. Almost overnight, being a Pakistani Muslim in New York became dangerous, and we had little choice but to move on. As a result I found myself in St. Albans, England. While I certainly understood the reasons for leaving New York, the infuriating emotions of having to start over yet again would not budge.

Worse was to come, however, when no English schools were prepared to accept me. At the age of sixteen, British students are due to complete their two-year syllabus and write their General Certificate of Secondary Education (GCSE) exams. That meant I had less than sixteen weeks in which to assimilate two years' worth of education, including completing the coursework and revising it for the final examinations. No school was prepared to accept those odds, which left me facing rejection after rejection.

All this upheaval, and the feelings of frustration and confusion that came with it, were tearing me up inside. I was tired of the pain – of the sheer anguish, guilt, and general disappointment with life. That was until one night when I woke up in a cold sweat at 3:14 am. I remember vividly the red numbers on the digital clock staring back at me in the quiet darkness. I was unsure what was going on, but I felt unusually calm and happy. It felt like something had shifted, and before I knew it, an automatic dialogue began within me.

"Is this the story I want to live for the rest of my life? Is this the person I want to be, especially with two younger sisters? Most certainly not. I want to be someone they can look to in order to realize that they don't have to be prisoners of the aftereffects of what happened to us all; that they, too, can change their beliefs. For some reason I feel that I have a duty to them, not to tell them how to live their lives, but to at least show them what is possible. Yet if I hold on to this story, I'm just going to replicate what I've been through. The events may vary, but the emotional turmoil won't. More important, I may not become the role model I aspire to be, or the person that my sisters see as an example of possibilities and that my brother and my parents are proud of and admire for walking through the fire and coming out stronger and courageous on the other side. What if I don't emerge as this person that something deep down inside me believes I can become?"

That's when I decided, "No! The future does not equal the past." I just knew I had to let go of my previous emotional experiences. I consciously decided that I would seek out any teacher, mentor, lessons, seminars, or trainings I could get my hands on and begin projecting a new vision and a new energy into my future.

I didn't (and still don't) know where that realization came from, but that wasn't important. All I knew was that my future did not have to mirror my past. I let go of focusing on the disempowering story in which I felt I was a victim, as if being ravaged by wolves tearing at my skin and pulling me in opposite directions. Instead I began to view these events as advantages, occurrences that pushed me so far that I had to come out fighting. So far, in fact, that I had to wake up from all the things I had been programmed to believe and follow. I started to create a new story.

Rather than viewing my start in American schooling as an exercise in alienation and inadequacy, I concentrated instead on the fact that despite speaking very limited English, I had worked my way from the bottom of the class to honors status within two years through nothing but stubborn determination. While some choose to blame a whole community for the acts of a few, I remembered my true friends who stood by me irrespective of my color and faith.

Success breathed new life into me and showed me that my way did work. I listened to my heart and persevered along my desired course, which afforded me a success that every school headmaster in the area had believed I couldn't achieve. One determined sixteen-year-old had proved them all wrong when I completed my GCSEs with top grades in less than four months.

My stomach no longer turns to ice as I recall rubbing my eyes, wakened groggy and confused by the cold sensation of a man holding a pistol to my temple. No longer do those four masked and armed men hold my heart and soul hostage with fear. I turned that sense of terror and dread into fearsome determination. No longer would I be controlled by another person. Instead I decided to take charge of my own life, which allowed me to live fully from my heart, to love passionately, and to simply put a smile on a stranger's face.

I know it won't be an easy journey. What if my new passions and directions no longer resonate with those I have picked up from my parents, my friends, culture, and society? Will I end up hurting the well-meaning people in my life who love me so dearly? Yes, that is a possibility. It is also possible to practice my courage and allow this to be one of those occasions in which selfishness trumps service. I can't serve anyone if I myself have not explored the foreign territory that lies ahead of me, inviting me to come and dig my hands in the earth and feel the cold, fresh, crumbly dirt through my fingers.

If I allow myself to live my past story and be controlled by the things I ought to and should do, then regret and bitterness will eat away at me and I will be of no use to anyone.

The ocean always grows calm after a storm, right? So let's embrace that moment to take in the serenity of calm and the still sea. A moment when there is no mind, no history, no fear, no pain... just peace. A moment when by surrendering to the power within us, we have opened a set of doors for pure, heartfelt inspiration to pour through.

Our busy and demanding lifestyles can easily lead to feelings of being overwhelmed, uncertainty, and stagnation. By focusing on both the inner game and the outer game of personal productivity, Mehrish Khan provides coaching with concrete solutions for transforming uncertainty and feelings of being overwhelmed into an integrated system of stress-free productivity. Visit www.Stress2Productivity.com to receive her FREE video series and learn how to decrease your daily distractions and accomplish more with your time.

Born Free

Nadine Love, MA

"YOU'RE PUTTING YOUR BABY'S LIFE AT RISK. This isn't about just jeopardizing your own life anymore." Dr. Parnell's hand trembled slightly as she pushed the pen into my steady hand. "If you insist on going ahead, you'll have to sign this."

Never had I been more certain. The silver pen was poised in the air like a dart while I read the fine print.

Dr. Parnell took the opportunity to continue. Her monologue seemed aimed at the corner of the room, not at me. "You're advised to take the more responsible option: have a Cesarean section. With the tumor behind your eye, there's no knowing the damage that will happen when you push. If the baby lives, and you... "

"I already explained. I'm not doing the traditional push. I've learned ..."

Dr. Parnell cut in. "The cranium is a sealed unit. You're a stroke candidate. My records show you had a stroke in November of 2000. There's your age. With the added complication of the tumor ..."

I signed the document. I'd just agreed to take on sole liability for my life, and that of my unborn child, against medical advice.

"Mind you arrange for the rescue helicopter to be on alert. You'll have to get a temporary landing permit."

I'd already made my application. I was well aware of the precautions necessary when living on an isolated seventeen-acre farm on an island.

Mira leveled a kick that caught me under the ribs. I relaxed, strangely reassured by the reminder of the individuality of the baby in my belly. I needed that! Seeing the words in print had unnerved me.

Theresa walked in. She was a friend and fellow organic vineyard owner with two young boys. Her younger son, Elton, had been home-birthed. Theresa was sure to be an ally.

"Nadine, you need to be sensible," she said, to my surprise. "You have that thing in your eye. You're not still thinking of having her at home are you? Too risky. Crazy. What does Bug say?"

"Bug" Steptoe was the island midwife. I went to see her. Her cheeks were redder than usual as she ushered me in. I thought it best to name it. "Been on the phone to Dr. Parnell?"

Bug nodded. "Much as this isn't what I want to do, I have to advise you against a home birth. I know how much you want a natural birth on the farm, but you really are safer and better off to have a C-section at the National Women's Hospital. Your age is a concern anyhow, even if you had no other potentially life-threatening conditions."

"So how do I exercise my right to choose? I'm going to birth her naturally, in tranquility, on the farm, in water, with no medication, and no invasive interventions. Are you saying you won't be involved?"

Bug gave a half-smile of reassurance. It wasn't much, but it was something. "I have to tell you we don't recommend this."

Mira adjusted her position. Comforting.

I read the coldly written fine print of Bug's legal disclaimer, feeling queasy and not letting on. I put my signature to the document, suddenly exhausted.

In what seemed to take forever, I reached the top of our hill and waddled the winding five-hundred-meter path to the front door. The phone was ringing. I lurched through the entrance and grabbed for the receiver, hoping perhaps it was my oldest friend, Elaine, or someone supportive. It was my mother.

"If that's what Dr. Parnell and Bug recommends, you're a fool to …" I hung up the phone.

When my husband returned, his response was still more discouraging: utter disinterest. When pressed, he snapped, "Do whatever you like." He left the next day on a trip to China to meet with one of his "Internet ladies."

At thirty-six weeks, Mira was confirmed to be in breech position with her extended legs and spine pointing to my left side. Like this, a natural birth would be impossible. With hypnosis, meditation, Reiki, and talking to her, Mira turned a third of the way.

I decided to have a procedure called an External Cephalic Version, in which a specialist lays hands on the abdomen and the baby can sometimes be turned.

This is administered normally with a painkiller. I had the procedure. No medication. I wanted no drug to affect Mira. I worked with active breathing, visualization, and Reiki. The procedure was successful, as I knew it would be.

Valentine's Day, 2006. The cool rush of predawn brushed my skin with champagne-bubble delight. Today was the day Mira would be born.

A soft, brown owl sat on the deck, looking directly at me – so close I could reach out and touch him. I could make out the fine veins of his feathers and the grey and brown flecks in his yellow eyes. I laid my right hand on my belly, sharing the experience with Mira, silently communicating to her that for her special day an owl had come to bid her welcome. When he took to his hushed flight, he flew toward me, gifting me a light caress on my cheek with his wingtip. I returned indoors, elated.

Floating bowls of candles, crystals, and flowers were prepared, ready to light. Oil burners were set with oils. Our large, round spa bath had been built so that the doors of the room opened onto the deck.

The joyous time came. I languished in the water, laughed, sucked watermelon ice, and made faces at Bug, who relaxed at the side of the spa. I breathed with the rhythm of my body. I glowed, complete, and in harmony with Mira's journey.

At 4:04 pm, in a kneeling squat, in the warm water, I sang out a "ho" and drew my baby girl upward, receiving her into my own arms. She was luminous. Born on a full moon, could she be other than Mira Moonbeam?

Fully present and triumphant, I cut the umbilical cord with the blessing: "You shine your light. I will always be here for you."

Mira Moonbeam was not the only one conceived at her rugged inception.

Through the process of deciding how I wanted to welcome my daughter into the world, I had to recommit to how I wanted to be in the world. The woman, the warrior, and the powerful mother were born in me at that time. The transformation enabled me to close the gate on a life in which I had held myself captive. I ended my marriage. I was free.

I stood my ground against a medical model that conspires to remove the right of women to be fear-free at a time when they deserve to be honored and empowered for the miraculous process of carrying and birthing a child.

I researched, prepared, and educated myself fully. I was fit.

I continue to take sole responsibility for my life. I've designed a total reset. I cleared the beliefs that brought on life-threatening illness, sabotaged my successes, and crushed close relationships. I've worked with the best mentors in the world. I've up-skilled to be at the leading edge of strategy creation for personal transformation. The tumor behind my eye "mysteriously" calcified, and my eyesight has been fully restored.

I have a blessed relationship with a man who supports my independence, growth, and commitment to service excellence. He's an involved, loving father to Mira. Together we answer a shared calling to contribute from our consciousness to our community.

I love my life as an Neuro-Linguistic Programming (NLP) trainer, mentor, and author. My days are filled with mothering Mira (who is now a flourishing five-year-old), and supporting others to find passion, purpose, and prosperity.

The way I approached Mira's birth became "My Sacred Seven-Step Blueprint for Happiness and Success." Here it is for you, so you can enjoy transformation more easily without making the mistakes I made along the way:

1. Be you. Back yourself. Decide on what you want. Work on your beliefs and values to ensure they support achieving your heart's true desire.

2. Never sell out on the core of who you are.

3. Find your personal mission and purpose. Measure all your decisions against these and you'll remain aligned.

4. Educate yourself thoroughly, on all levels (practically and metaphysically).

5. Have an open mind and an open heart, while knowing when to say no. Cultivate flexibility.

6. Be brave and bold in backing yourself by taking action consistently.

7. Be fully present. All we have is unfolding moments of now.

8. Be generous and grateful. Give and receive love.

I make a stand for you to find your magnificence and to be that fully. Be true to yourself and find your own magnificence.

Love yourself. Love what you do. Make your difference.

Nadine Love, MA, is a prizewinning transformational author, celebrated international speaker, award-winning trainer, and motivational mentor. With twenty-five years' experience in the international wellness industry, she is acclaimed for facilitating rapid and lasting change. Nadine enables people to live their boldest dreams and to make their unique difference. She is passionate about contributing to a resilient, peaceful, conscious global community. Visit www.NadineLove.com for Your FREE video/audio download of Nadine's empowering message: "Be You, Be Magnificent: A Blueprint."

From Soul Searching to Soul Singing: Trusting, Transforming, and Thriving

Olivia Lobell

THERE I WAS, CELEBRATING the completion of my Master's Degree in London, UK – a dream of mine coming true – after many aspiring years of deeply desiring it, enjoying the fruits of my success in being a Master Teacher. So why was I trapped in an inner emptiness, feeling uneasy and unclear, and experiencing a sense of disconnection from the inside out? Why was I struggling to enjoy my successful language teaching career, with my head and heart surrounded by confusion, concerns, and worries about the years to come?

I felt I didn't know what I wanted, nor did I desire to work in a nine-to-five job anymore, which made me feel even more overwhelmed and frustrated. I was unbalanced, asking myself, "Who am I? Why am I here? Why do I feel so empty while I have such success?" The gap between my outer success experience and the inner world of myself was really huge.

Something was missing, and I have now discovered what that something was — it was me and my soul! I was unawakened, living my life unconsciously, without purpose. Although in many respects I had been very successful, I was completely lost inside. My authentic self was not only largely absent, but also starving and screaming to be heard in my daily life. Because I was doing what I thought I was supposed to do, I was getting and achieving a lot, but I was still not as fulfilled as I desired to be, and the authentic me was struggling.

In early 2009 I discovered personal development, and began a self-discovery stage in my life — what I call my "soul searching" journey. It was definitely a turning point in my professional and personal life. I immersed myself deeply in self-growth, and with the support of my precious husband, I was able to invest my time, money, and energy in as many books, courses, and home study programs as I could.

By the end of that year I discovered professional coaching, and I was over the moon. I realized that I had been teaching, training, mentoring, and (informally) coaching students, professionals, family, and friends for so many years, but I didn't know about coaching as a professional career. I happily exclaimed to myself, "Oh my goodness, there is a profession for my passion, my purpose. I can't believe it!" It was everything I wanted to do… to help others succeed in life by following their dreams, passion, and purpose, and create a life they love.

At that very moment, I made a commitment to immerse myself in absolutely everything that had to do with professional coaching and to build a successful, thriving business. Again, I read every book on coaching, business, marketing, and mindset I could get my hands on. I went to every seminar, workshop, and course that was available. I essentially decided to become an expert in personal transformation and business growth, and I eventually became a specialist in authentic business and marketing success.

The whole process was magical and truly transformational, because I remembered as a child and young adult I'd always felt as if there was something inside me that wanted to come alive. I knew I had something special to share, that I wanted to make a difference and a contribution to the world. Now I know that I had felt a deep calling in my youth, but at that time I was unaware of it. After all, I was a day and night dreamer, always dreaming big dreams, and everyone around me really seemed to be entertained by them.

At the age of twenty-three I decided to follow one of my biggest dreams: to travel to the United States, and for the first time I would be away from my hometown, Rosario do Sul, in the south of Brazil. I was completely thrilled and very happy indeed. I was following my heart, and I so thoroughly enjoyed the time I lived and studied in Florida. I felt deep inside that I didn't want to stay in Brazil anymore. Instead, I wanted to travel the world, explore new cultures, new possibilities, and different ways of living. Regrettably, I returned back to my place of birth.

When I was getting ready to go back to the United States in 2001, my father fell ill, and then September 11th happened. It was a dramatic and suffering year for the world, and for my family and me because my father had cancer. His illness and subsequent death was devastating for all of us. After his passing, I felt that calling again – my inner voice telling me it was time to follow my heart once more and live my dreams of travelling, living abroad, and exploring the world. I paid attention and listened to it, and just two weeks after my dad's departure from this life, I moved to London, UK, in January of 2002.

My adventure in London was a journey of wonderful exploration. I met my twin soul and got married in 2004, travelled to over twelve countries in Europe, and enjoyed the time I spent with my husband's family in Italy.

By the end of 2008, I finished my Master's Degree and had my deepest wake-up call. This time was different. I realized that the inner emptiness I was feeling was my soul screaming out in divine discontent, saying to me, "You have a unique purpose to follow. Discover your true, authentic self, and follow your biggest dreams, deepest desires, and authentic aspirations. Only do what you passionately love and what makes you feel purposeful, meaningful, and fulfilled." I had learned to listen carefully to my inner voice – my authentic self – and act on it despite my fears, concerns, and anxieties. I began to pay close attention to who I truly wanted to become, what I really wanted to do, and what I authentically wanted to create in my life.

I now feel incredibly blessed to have discovered my purpose. I am living my passion, following my heart, doing what I love, and my soul is singing again. It is such a blessing and joy to build and grow my own business, and to inspire, empower, and enlighten others to discover their blessing, passion, and purpose and to bring to being their best selves – their authentic selves – and to help these passionate professionals create the business and life they've always dreamed of.

My message is simple, but very powerful and profound. You are here for a reason: to be of service, to give and receive, and to truly thrive. So be who you truly are destined to be, do the work you were born to do, share the message you were meant to share, and make the difference you are here to make, by following your heart, listening to your soul, and doing what you love.

By being authentically successful doing what you love, you will make your soul sing. Therefore, I invite you to pay close attention to these three transformational tools:

1. Start small, but dream BIG, and believe in your dreams no matter what.

2. Follow your heart, listen to your soul – your authentic voice – and act on what really matters to you despite your fears, obstacles, and doubts.

3. Connect with and create who you truly want to become – the best version of your authentic you – and fulfill what you are here to fulfill.

In a nutshell, trust your intuition and your inspiration, and **be who you dream** of being so that you can transform, transcend, and truly thrive!

From my own experience, one of the best ways to share your unique transformation, and make a bigger impact and income doing what you love, is to build your own authentic business and become an enlightened entrepreneur. It gives you freedom of full self-expression, autonomy to take control of your own life and destiny, and most important, a sense of meaning, fulfillment, and joy to align your energy with your true power, passion, and purpose.

I hope my experience, knowledge, words, and wisdom resonate with your heart and soul, light the way for you to succeed in life on your own terms, and inspire you to transform and truly thrive, starting today. If so, you are in the right place, at the right time, with the right mentor, and I am here to let you know that the right way to enjoy the journey is to align your inner world with your outer world and create authentic abundance from the inside out.

I invite you to join us on this incredible, joyful journey to awaken the enlightened entrepreneur within. Just think and feel how much richer and purer this world will be when you trust and uncover the true, authentic potential that lies inside you. You will become empowered and transformed, and truly thrive together with this transformational tribe of authentic awakening souls.

Let's enjoy the universal energetic spiritual journey and have more fulfillment, freedom, and fun, shall we?

Olivia Lobell is the founder of Authentic Business Success and the author of *The Enlightened Entrepreneur*. Walking her talk, Olivia went from a soul-searching journey in her life to building a successful, thriving business she loves. Through her transformational books, live events, and coaching and mentoring programs, she teaches passionate professionals how to become enlightened entrepreneurs and make a bigger impact and income doing what they love. To get your FREE Authentic Business Success training, visit www.AuthenticBizSuccess.com.

The Environment Connection
and Oneness of All There Is

Regina E. H–Ariel

"ONE SMALL PART OF A PRECIOUS LIFE."

In the early nineties I joined an international gathering of "lightwork-ers" in French Polynesia. The journey consisted of a round trip to several islands: Moorea, Huahine, Bora Bora, and Tahiti. The purpose of the gath-ering was planetary healing and the opening of the birth canal for Mother Earth and all life to move into the 5th dimensional realm of truth and the "Golden Age."

We prepared for this special event over four days. This special ceremony took place within the ocean waters. The participants formed two parallel lines, creating a water canal between us. Singing mantras and starry songs, we created an energy field of "oneness." Floating on our backs, we passed through this canal one by one, moved gently by the hands of the participants.

One of the staff members arrived late, and instead of settling down first, he playfully entered the canal with his diving equipment on. Some of the participants began laughing, and before he had passed the half-way mark, the sacred energy field of oneness broke into pieces, shifting it into a mixture of fun, confusion, and helplessness that we did not know what to do with or how to save the situation.

Some of us tried to hold everything together, but the attempt was in vain. That was a hard moment for the leader, as we had "failed." She turned away and left the water in an angry mood, leaving many in a state of shock. The ceremony area filled with powers of deception and anger mixed with guilt, shame, and sadness. The birth canal was destroyed, and nobody knew what do.

I was not prepared for such a reaction among lightworkers, and was in a kind of energy shock. So I went to the beach, close to our holy stone circle, to sit down, meditate, talk to God, and work with the heavenly realms to forgive and to neutralize those energies and re-create peace and harmony.

The beach sloped gently to the water, and I sat down, pulling my knees very close to my body, holding them with my arms, looking over the endless ocean. In a meditative and deeply relaxed state, I stretched my left arm out, drawing a circle in the sand halfway around my body. Without thinking, I did the same with my right arm and finished sitting in a closed circle. It felt good and safe, sitting like a Native American, embracing myself in this tiny space within my personal circle.

Breathing into the divine within, I entered my "inner point zero" – the portal to the oneness of all there is. While working to re-harmonize the group energy in communion with God and the angelic realms, the vibration of the sand I was sitting on caught my attention. Adapting to that vibration underneath my body, I felt it getting stronger with each breath. Somehow I opened up to a level at which individuality disappears. Sitting, watching inside, feeling, hearing, and sensing wave after wave bringing their vibrations through the sand, the energy became heavy, and I had to put my head down on my knees. The power of the ocean waves entered my body, each time stronger, until I was totally filled with its sound and vibration. I let it happen while observing and praying for peace and harmony.

I grew and expanded until I merged completely with the ocean and all the waters in this world. I felt the atomic and subatomic vibrations of my being. I was everywhere in each drop of salty water, in the depth of the deepest places. I felt all kinds of fish inside my being, all kinds of underwater sea life, a wonder of variety. I felt the dolphins playing inside me as the water of life. I felt the I AM, the joy, the happiness of creatures in harmony. Any kind of disturbing energies in the group were just swept away in this holy union.

My physical body began to feel incredibly heavy, and at the same time my being was so free, so clear, purified, and holy. It was such a blessing to feel the vastness of the water and to be in total oneness with the great power of life. The feeling of being so small in a human body and so huge at the same time opened my being to a higher frequency of understanding life itself and the powers we carry inside. This oneness was real, not a dream or my imagination. It was pulsating inside my blood and my muscles, and in each atom of my being. I felt my aura expanding and vibrating to a level that cannot be described in words, as it comes with deepness and divine happiness that no one can imagine exists until they experience it for themselves.

Suddenly a thought entered my mind: "How do I get out of this vastness of the one energy field that is everywhere?" I was everywhere, and I was not able to move my physical body. How should I shrink myself again to fit into this tiny body? I tried, but nothing worked. I was the ocean, I was the sand, I was all of life. How could I be a human being and also all that is?

The lords of the winds and the lords of the waters welcomed me home. I was overwhelmed by so much honor and grace for this experience. At the same time, the energy began to feel too overpowering, as I became a channel of love for releasing planetary negativity.

When I was close to falling over and leaving my body, I sensed somebody at my left side. I do not know how, but for a brief second I focused on that, and lifted my head to look at the additional vibration. A member of the group was standing close to my circle, and he asked me what I was doing there, sitting in that small space. Still dizzy, I said, "Thanks. You just saved my life. I was about to cross over while sitting in this position." Tears of joy and grace ran down my face. "It just happened. I was working on peace in the group, and merged with the ocean."

He told me that he had been living in India for several years, and that Master Yogis and Rishis go into the deep forest for self-purification from time to time. They sit in the same way I was sitting: inside a circle they draw around themselves for protection. I already knew at that time that I had had several lifetimes in India, and it showed me how knowledge is stored on a cellular level, becoming available the moment we need it. Our subconscious remembers, and we just use the inner wisdom without having any conscious idea about the meaning in this lifetime, until we're reminded by an event, situation, or place that awakens us to the deeper truth of life. Speaking with him helped me to bring all the vastness back into my body, and I was happy that Source had sent me physical help in the form of a dear friend.

In the next session we had, all negativity was gone, and the harmony reached a much higher level than before. The leader opened a peace ceremony and asked for forgiveness for each one of us in the circle. Tears of love and joy sealed the harmony, which grew into a field of divine oneness that was very powerful. This time the ceremony happened at a very deep and powerful level, and we accomplished our mission successfully.

This experience taught me that things that appear negative at first have a bigger picture behind them. The first time our group was not strong enough to hold the new frequencies for rebirthing a new spiral of evolution, so something had to happen to create the powerful energies that would be able to hold the vibration of the planetary shift during the transformational process.

I experienced true oneness and how the power of divine love can shift negativity and pain within a short time — how it can heal places, regions, and people. It reminded me that time is an illusion, and that we carry all the wisdom of all lifetimes within. I was shown that when we are totally committed and open for divine love, we become an instrument of transformation for all life. When we open up to higher service, every day is blessed with miracles.

This experience was such a blessing, and transformed me into a being with galactic alignments and universal understanding. It was my conscious birthing process of the "One I AM," the alignment of my own divine mission on earth in oneness with source, and a seal of commitment and dedication as a divine instrument of love.

May all readers find access to that sacred Oneness and discover divinity within as a normal state of being.

Blessings.

Regina E. H-Ariel is devoted to the "Eternal One" and Multi-Dimension Global Education. She is a Transformational Multi-Dimensional Quantum Healer, Intuitive Soul Healer, Spiritual Psychologist & Life Coach, Transformational Author, Artist, and Speaker at Life Events. She is dedicated to the process of accelerated awakening to Divine Consciousness, Universal Understanding, and Oneness. She is Co-Founder of Diamond Light Ascension — Sacred Site Tours & Journeys — decoding the "Diamond Light Matrix Within," activating the Divine Self. Visit www.2ThePowerOfSpirit6.com, www.ArielAngelArtAndPhotography.com, or www.DiamondLightAscension.com.

Becoming a Clear Conduit
for Transformation

Robert G. Allen

THERE ARE CERTAIN DAYS in your life that get indelibly imprinted in your brain and totally change your life. March 15th, 2003, is one that will stay with me forever.

I was due to speak to 1000 people at the Anaheim Convention Center that day, and it had been a long one. I had flown in from a speech I had given in Oregon and was totally wiped. I had been working on my presentation until at least midnight when I accidentally pushed a button and lost all my PowerPoint presentation. So I stayed up until four or five o'clock in the morning, caught a plane, and arrived in Anaheim to talk to this group of people.

After speaking, my staff said, "You look tired. Can we drive you home?" I'm a pretty independent man and I said no. It was raining out and there were a lot of car accidents that night up and down the freeways of California, and mine was one of them. I veered off the road at about nine o'clock at night and met a large oak tree face-to-face at high speed. Next thing I knew,

I woke up in the hospital and, as they say, "the rest is history." My life changed in that moment.

Before my near fatal car crash, I was much less connected to my heart. That accident transformed my life. Frankly I can't think about it without starting to cry – it was a very profound experience. I had a broken back, a broken wrist, and all kinds of major injuries that still hurt today, but you know, I wouldn't give back that accident for all the money in the world.

After my car accident, I began to truly realize how short life is. I started feeling like I had to start doing things more quickly and not "waste" my time. I wanted to get everything in! So I climbed Mount Kilimanjaro in Africa, with a bad leg, and did a few other things because I was determined to pack as much living as possible into a short period of time.

On the way back home from climbing the tallest mountain in Africa, which was a profound transformational experience in itself, my family and I stopped in Amsterdam. I was out one day, just wandering the streets, when a guy dashed out of a café on one of the canals, ran up to me, and introduced himself as one of my readers. He said, "I'm here with my family because a book you wrote transformed my life. Now I'm financially free, and I'm traveling around the world with my family. I just wanted to thank you." He shook my hand and left me standing there stunned! That's what happens when a book that was destined to be written falls into the hands of someone who was meant to read it.

To share your greatest gifts in life, it's essential to become a conduit for a higher power or whatever word you wish to use: God, Universe, Source. The truth of the matter is you never know what kind of impact your actions or words will have on others. This is the power of tossing a pebble in the pond – the ripples expand to places beyond your imagination.

The thing with being a conduit for grace to flow through you and serve others, your conduit needs to be clear and clean. If your conduit is closed or cloudy, then this energy from which your greatest insights and wisdom come will be blocked, and you won't be able to share what you're here to share.

Some people refer to that inner "closed" voice as your ego, but I prefer to call it a critical voice. Over the years, I've come to understand that that voice is a liar; it doesn't want me or you to win. If you give a lot of attention to it, then it shuts you down.

Had my critical voiced taken over when I was lying in the hospital bed recovering, I'd never be where I am today. I could have ended up feeling sorry for myself rather than being grateful to be alive and even more passionate about helping other people experience the success they desire.

And I'm telling you that critical voice can get very loud sometimes. So try to tune your "hearing" in to the subtler, softer, more friendly sound of your true voice.

If you constantly get a barrage of negativity from your critical voice, you'll find yourself being disconnected from your source of power, and it will literally shut you down. This is a very difficult place to be in when you desire to make a difference in the world.

As you learn how to deal with the critical voice and take it off of the playing field of your mind so that your mind is clear, you'll be ready to receive the messages you are meant to share with others. You want to get to the space that Neuro-Linguistic Programming (NLP) practitioners call "up-time." It's as if your sub-conscious mind has been switched to "on," and amazing thoughts, even genius ones, simply flow through you so fast that you can hardly keep up with them. That is the place from which you ultimately want to live and create.

One thing I do that you may want to consider, too, is read a spiritual or scriptural book in the morning to tap in to the wisdom of the ages, and then I say a kneeling prayer during which I clear my mind out so I'm more receptive to grace and guidance. My prayers are not the kind in which I ask for something specific for myself, but rather I ask how I can help. They're more like saying, "Look at the Universe You've created. It's unbelievable. You've got things to do on this planet! How can I help You? Who do I need to talk to today? How can I be a source of light that needs to be shed on this fairly dark world? When I speak, how can I say the words You want me to say?"

I stay kneeling until I feel a connection — when I know I'm communicating with my heavenly Father. It's a very profound and deeply spiritual experience that I try to have as often as I can. It doesn't happen every day, but I do my best. When I am ready to communicate, whether verbally or written, I say, "Please open up my mind and my heart and let Your wishes flow through me."

To me this is the path to transformation. It is not fireworks. It is not the bells and whistles. It is not the big stage. It is not accomplishing some big goal in your life. The path to transformation occurs inside of you in the quietest of moments, perhaps brought on by a trauma or a challenge (like my car crash was for me).

Before my accident, I was very closed. I wasn't willing to share these thoughts as openly as I am now because I was afraid I would offend somebody's spiritual sensibilities. I was worried about what people might think. When you have a near-death experience, you don't worry anymore about what people think; you just say what you know you're supposed to say because you don't know how long you're going to get to say it.

Fear is one of those things you have to clear out of your conduit first to get the critical voice out of your head, and then turn on the true voice of your heart. The true voice is a message you feel that comes in words, but you actually "feel" the meaning behind them. The critical voice is a mind thing — a from-the-neck-up kind of thinking — and the heart part is when you speak directly from your heart. When you're speaking from your heart, people get it, even if it might be slightly different from their own personal beliefs. They get that you're coming from a heart space.

The metaphor I like to use to explain the difference between these two modes is this: Imagine that you are a tuning fork. When you are on tune to perfect pitch and speaking your true message, it resonates with others who are meant to hear it. Another way of saying it is to sing your greatest song, and others will sing with you. I think it was Thoreau who said, most men lead lives of quiet desperation and go to the grave with their song still in them. Our job, as people who want to make a positive difference in the world and send out those waves of transformation, is to sing that song in perfect pitch to the best of our ability!

And those who are destined to hear, read, or be touched in some way by your message will start to vibrate at the tone you're sending out – just like a tuning fork can cause other tuning forks nearby to resonate and vibrate at that exact same pitch. The positive resonance your message strikes with others causes them to vibrate with the same sense of joy, of purpose. That's when a global transformation begins to take place.

Always keep your conduit clean and act on those nudges you receive. Remember: The more YOU open up and pass along the messages you are told to share, the more the world will open up for you.

Robert G. Allen is one of America's most famous and most influential financial advisors. After receiving his MBA from Brigham Young University in 1974, Allen began his real estate investment career and turned his successful experiences into the colossal bestselling book, *Nothing Down*, which spent fifty-eight weeks on the *New York Times* bestseller list. Four other major *New York Times* bestsellers – *Creating Wealth*, *Multiple Streams of Income*, *The One Minute Millionaire*, and *Cracking the Millionaire Code* – soon followed. His latest book with co-author Mark Victor Hansen is *Cash in a Flash: Fast Money in Slow Times*. You can learn more about Robert Allen and his programs by visiting www.RobertAllen.com.

How Pain Taught Me LOVE

Dr. Rose GS

IT WAS A CHALLENGING YEAR FOR ME, 1997. I knew I was tested and tried with the mighty fall of my "Love Castle," a wonderful marriage that seemed was going to end at any time. I had no one to turn to except God. Well, who else could I actually turn to in a time like this?

After three years of going through what seemed like hell on earth, one fateful night I asked God a question – not in anger, but in tears, and in all sincerity wanting to know. I just wanted my answer. I asked Him, "Dear God, please tell me why I have to go through this pain. Have I done something that angered You? I know I might have, but please don't punish me like this. Please forgive me. Please let me know why I have to go through such pain."

Immediately after that prayer, I cried myself to sleep, which was no different from all the other nights for those three long years.

But that night my prayers were answered in the most vivid dream I have ever had. In that dream, I saw from the back a beautiful lady standing on a tall stage. She looked radiant with so much love. Thou-

232

sands of people from all over the world had come to hear her speak. Her energy was so sweet, and I felt so much love exuding from her. I could feel that her eyes gleamed with so much adoration that when she looked into the eyes of those who came to meet and hear her speak, it was enough to heal their pains.

As I stared in awe, looking at this wonderful person, I heard a thundering voice addressing me from another direction. I did not question what or whose voice it was; I just knew and trusted. The voice said, "You have to go through the pain for the leadership you have to take." Then, as if it had been signaled, the loving person on the stage turned to me, and to my surprise, that beautiful, loving lady I saw on that stage... was me!

Immediately upon realizing that, I awoke and returned to reality. I was shaking, perspiring, and in tears. I was very afraid in so many ways. Afraid that I might forget this dream, afraid that the dream was true, and also afraid that it was not true, because all of these thoughts had their own set of implications. I ran to my wardrobe across the room, frantically searched its drawers for a pen and paper, and quickly scribbled the last message I had heard.

And sure enough I could never forget those words. In fact, they live in me to this very day! They are still vivid in my mind, and burned into my soul, asking me to share them with as many people as I possibly can. They haunt me, push me, and remind me about one very important thing – the leadership I have to take!

"What leadership am I to take?" I asked myself with huge disbelief. And perhaps the biggest question of all that kept pushing its way into my head for years after that was, "Who am I to take any leadership?"

One day as I was driving and crying at the same time, thinking of my almost ruined marriage, a sense of self-pity and grief came over me. I was full of shame, and my self-esteem was very much battered. I remember thinking, "How am I to face the world? How am I to continue living?" I remember taking deep breaths many times, as my anger and sadness felt so overwhelming. To me, then, mighty was the fall of my so-called wonderful marriage. I remember that I kept telling myself many times that there must be something good that would come out of this suffering and misery.

Suddenly I heard a soft whisper. With all certainty, I just knew that I needed to listen to that voice. "Be the angel of love. Teach about love. Be the example. Lead and show the world." An image of a book came to me – "THE MESSAGE IS LOVE," it said. With that, I felt a deep knowing that I was to spread LOVE to the whole world. I believed, "That is the leadership that I need to take. And not just that, I am also to heal the hurts and unite the world." I was stunned and fearful. I remember thinking, "Me? A nobody? How am I to do that? Who am I to kid? Who am I to do such a thing?" I was in denial for many years, doubting myself and hating those whispers that I knew would definitely change my life.

From that moment, every time I was where there were many people I did not know, I would question myself, "Am I to love them? Am I to spread love to these people who I do not even know and don't even care about?" It looked like such an impossible and far-fetched idea that I was to spread love! And it looked even more impossible for me to be the "Angel of Love," as was whispered to me!

To make things worse, there was another voice that kept tormenting me, loud and clear, saying, "Who are you to lead? Who are you to write a book about LOVE? Who are you to even imagine you can spread love, let alone heal the hurts and unite the world, when your own love life is almost ruined?" Those words pierced into my mind and heart like a sharp dagger and brought me to another level of self-doubt and self-loathing. For many years I struggled to free myself from it.

Because this book is in your hands, I know that something drew us together for a purpose that will only be revealed as we walk the paths of our lives. Your path and mine are intertwined for a beautiful reason. I also know that your life's story is very important and needs to be told for others to benefit and learn from. In fact, that is why I am sharing this story with you; because I believe somehow it will strike a chord in your beautiful self, and it will give you the power to come forward and bring forth your GIFTS to the world. Maybe my role here is to remind you to listen to that voice inside of you that keeps reminding you of your gifts and greatness.

With that, allow me to gently ask you, "What are your gifts that you have forgotten? What are your dreams that you have allowed to be buried deep in your fears? What are your hurts that are calling for **LOVE** to come and heal you – the ones you have denied?" Know that your gifts and your talents are there so that they shine onto others and you, showering all with **LOVE** and **HOPE**. Your hurts and pains are the golden bridge to those hearts that you are to help heal and set free. They will unleash your beautiful strength in order to bring out the YOU who is needed to lead and shine along the path of those who are still blinded by their hurts and pains.

Today eleven years have passed since the worst yet most illuminating time of my life. I am blessed to see that as my life unfolds, I am becoming more like the woman in my dream. I weathered the hurricane in my marriage, and both my husband and I have rebuilt it with an even greater love. We are so grateful that the learning has allowed us to have a blissful marriage now. Opportunities come for me to spread the message of love and to heal and empower individuals whose pain had paralyzed them. And what a wonderful feeling it is to be able to witness how they recover and become the ambassadors of love themselves who bring a ripple effect to their families, workplaces, and the communities in which they live.

After more than a decade since that dream, one thing I realize is that this world needs more love than ever. The world has become more and more chaotic because too many of its occupants operate from a lack of love that was passed down from generation to generation and has resulted in undesirable ways of living. And the way I see it, LOVE is the answer to all problems, because all problems are caused by the lack of it, including the economic challenges that the world is facing now. Love is a very important word, yet the most misunderstood. The challenge is for us to operate from the place of love in this seemingly unlovely world. When you and I, the individuals who make up organizations, communities, countries, and the world, can operate from the place of love, know that joy, happiness, and harmony will be the result.

Looking back, I fully realize and am grateful that my most trying time was actually the most wonderful gift from God. It has transformed me and taught me love and its expansiveness, because hidden in it is the wonderful message of love from Him who showed me who I AM. I believe you, too, will soon find your darkest time to be the torch illuminating your walk of life. And when you embrace this, you will find serenity and total peace. My wish for you: May love always shine on your path.

Dr. Rose GS, is currently engaged in her project "The Message Is Love" to spread love globally. For more than twenty-two years this love advocator has been sharing, teaching, and empowering individuals and corporations on the power of love through her seminars, courses, and writings. Her expansive understanding of love has inspired, motivated, and transformed thousands of people to live an enriched and balanced life. For more information, visit www.DrRoseGS.com or www.MessageIsLove.com.

Transformation in My Hand

Sandra Longmore

THE AIR, THICK WITH SUSPENSE, was punctuated by a throbbing sound in my ears. It was the hammering beat of my heart as it pumped out of my control. Everything stopped, frozen in time. I could hear an inner voice whispering to me, "You are here. This is it the moment you have been waiting for. Choose again now."

This was an extraordinary moment when I could feel transformation was close, so immediate that I felt certain I could feel it in the palm of my hand.

It was while writing this chapter that I had this feeling. I could see myself standing in the moonlight before a beautiful, transparent, clear pond. As I looked at the pond's shimmery clear surface, I could feel grace and possibility waiting below the surface. Looking down at my hand, I was surprised to see a smooth pebble, and even more surprising was that I knew exactly what to do. I stood up straight, proudly swung my arm back, and then swiftly launched my pebble up into the air. It went higher than I could ever imagine and came down with a splash that caused mirroring ripples to spread out in a gentle wave that touched the Creator's heart.

I looked around me and saw many others also throwing pebbles in the water. I know that they, too, heard the call to come to this master heart pond.

You see, I am a creative visionary coach, and I collect these special moments that align with the possibility for transformation.

You might come to the point of transformation because you are tired of the struggle. The spark has gone out of your soul, and nothing feels good anymore. You have invested endless amounts of time in projects and are so full of information that you feel your brain will pop into a thousand pieces like popcorn in a popcorn popper.

This is my story in which my journey to being started. The struggle, the fatigue, and the new transformational vision all happened in 1990.

I was living in Washougal, Washington, on a mountain, with my husband, daughter, three lamas, a dog, and a cat. My husband, Tom, was always supportive of my desires, and though he did not like to talk about deep topics, I always felt his silent encouragement when I needed a lift.

Tom is from Long Beach, California, and had moved from the hustle and bustle of a fast-paced life to Washougal in exchange for adventure and a quieter life. He had picked several acres in the country for the perfect place to live, then designed and built the geodesic dome home where we were living. He had the foresight to make sure we had good water, and after the city tested it, they said we had the purest well water they had ever seen. Tom's philosophy is that if we have good water, nature, and adventure, we have a good life.

I was feeling discontented the day we left our dome home for a month-long trip to sell my Fine Art Apparel. Our country home was shrouded in overcast clouds. Rain was drizzling down my face and the air was thick with the smell of more to come. I felt as heavy and dark as the wet weather as I slammed the door on our Ford van shut and we slowly rolled down our driveway. I looked at my dome art studio with mixed feelings, and my heart twisted with confusion as a knot formed in my throat.

It had been such a delight when Tom first built the dome studio for me. Almost every morning I would walk out our front door and amble down the path and in through the front door of the workshop to begin creating my works of art. Every day for endless hours I painted... and painted... and painted. My business was called Sandra's Fine Art Apparel, and I painted on stylish garments and fabrics. I bought the finest materials I could find and hand dyed each one. On each garment I composed a masterpiece of art that was unique to each garment. They were spectacular works of art, but I was tired – very, very tired.

This trip was so we could sell what I had created. The month on the road passed slowly, and all I could think was "When will this be over?" At long last the month had finished, and as a reward we were going to vacation in Sedona, Arizona.

Sedona has a worldwide reputation for being a spiritual mecca and global power spot, and I wanted to go there. I imagined that a transformation of some kind would occur, and new thoughts began to take root in my mind. I was excited and ready for new experiences. I breathed in the word Sedona... I breathed out the word Sedona, and my mind was filled with positive expectations and beliefs. I was going to find one of the vortex spots where the masculine/electric up flows and the feminine/magnetic in flows meet, and set myself down on a blanket with a gallon of water and experience something wonderful. I could hardly contain my feelings of anticipation as this vision sparked in my mind's eye. I was ready to dive into those deeper dimensions and let my transformation soar beyond my dreams.

Driving through the high desert of Arizona we experienced mild weather and sunshine, and our lungs breathed in the clean air. As we approached the mouth of the spectacular Oak Creek Canyon, Tom began to speak very strangely.

He asked, "Honey, what would you do with your life if you had to do it all over again?" I was astonished to hear these words coming out of his mouth. I had waited our whole married life to discuss the deeper meaning of life with him. Whenever I talked of anything spiritual, psychological, or consciousness-raising, he suddenly had selective hearing. Now I thought I must have the same ailment. I couldn't possibly have heard those words coming from him, let alone the question of what I would do if I could start all over again. He then followed it up with another question, asking, "How would your world look? I really want to know what you think."

The only sense I could make of this conversation was that the magic of Sedona was working. The spiritual mecca had penetrated his brain and the vortex had magnetized his consciousness. He was speaking the words and sparking conversation in the direction I had always longed to go with him. He spoke again. "Tell me, would you continue painting on clothes? I know you are feeling pretty burned out and don't like having employees depend on you for their paychecks and their emotional problems."

That's all it took. I picked up the ball and started to run for a touchdown. I blurted out, "NO! No, I would not paint on clothes.

No, I would not have employees, and no, I would not do shows. I would paint on canvas. I would create differently. I would get a regular paycheck every week and develop my personal creative style. I would feel creative and alive again, not buried under the pile of all these garments. Even though they're very beautiful, they weigh me down."

The next words glided out of Tom's mouth as if in slow motion: "That... is... a... very... nice... vision... and... you... have... an... even... nicer... opportunity... now. You can follow that vision. You see, yesterday, during our Sacramento show, I got a call from Washougal. You were selling your clothes like hot cakes and making us lots of money, so I held back the message from the call until today. The call was from one of your employees. She was crying hysterically about how she had done something very, very bad. She had violated your rule to never leave the studio when the heaters were still on. During her absence, something happened and started a blaze. Your studio burned down yesterday. It went up like a rocket according to the neighbors who came for miles, attracted by the flames as they leaped into the air. That life you just described as being undesirable is gone and you get to live your new dream."

As I absorbed the information I had just heard, I saw my first red rock of Sedona, and to my amazement and confusion I felt the relief of having a huge burden leave my shoulders. My heart expanded into a new vision. I could not have designed this moment more perfectly with the greatest stage director and writers in the world. This was the sweet-spot moment in which I was so far down the path of vision that my current reality didn't matter.

Today I am living from that pivotal moment. I am a creative visionary coach, published author, Inspirational Speaker and

Teacher of creativity who gets lots of checks regularly written to her. I like to think of myself as a collector of these moments of transformation and change as I live my life of being fully alive.

Sandra Longmore is a Certified Life Coach, Law of Attraction Trainer, Vision Board Facilitator, Author, Speaker, and Artist. Sandra lives, laughs, and loves "outside the box." As a skillful coach and creative thinker, Sandra brings enthusiasm, energy, and transformation to her clients, audiences, and readers, inspiring them to live their best lives. Visit www.SandraLongmore. com to get your FREE discovery session.

One Hundred and Twenty Miles

Sandye Brown

"DEAR GOD, PLEASE HELP ME! Tonight I promise to go straight home, make myself a hearty meal, pay a few bills, and get a good night's sleep."

This had been my constant prayer every workday for six months into my new life. By now I was living in Montana, a transplanted African-American woman from New Jersey, making every attempt to forget about the life I had trashed. With my few meager belongings, I had packed my little Honda car and driven across the country. Seeing no way to salvage a respectable life, I had literally fled from broken friendships, embarrassing behaviors I couldn't remember having committed, and an intense despair arising from being morally, emotionally, and spiritually bankrupt.

If you have participated in any kind of twelve-step program, you can recognize the familiar lyrics of the song sung by one who is addicted to people, drugs, alcohol, food, or any other substance. In my case, I was at the height of my "career" as a drug-addicted alcoholic — out of control, profoundly lost, hopeless, and helpless.

I had begun drinking at age fourteen to help me cope with emotional, sexual, and physical abuse, complicated by a social phobia disorder that left me feeling overexposed and excessively vulnerable in public. Living with alcoholic parents, it was a no-brainer that drinking would be a natural coping strategy. And it worked well enough — for a time.

But nineteen years later, my well-constructed system of denial had slowly eroded. In its wake was the harsh reality that I had abdicated a life of joy, purpose, and connection by allowing drugs and alcohol to ascend to the throne of sovereignty in my life. When my denial cracked open, a desperate sense of urgency compelled me to run for my life. But as the saying goes, "Wherever you go, you take yourself with you."

And I knew that. But... I didn't *know* that.

I fully expected that with a clean slate — new people, no history — my geographical "cure" would be the magic pill to transform everything. I had deliberately moved to a very small town with a population of 100 to minimize the possibility of being seduced by "big city" life. Although the town had two bars, about a mile apart, I was certain that I could avoid them somehow. As could be predicted, within a few short weeks I had befriended the "cool" people, become a regular at my new favorite bar, and elevated the local pot dealer to boyfriend status. Hence the cycle continued with even greater vengeance.

My only saving grace at this time was that I was a "functional" addict. I was articulate and bright. I presented myself well and I had a good work ethic (meaning that I could show up for work every day). Consequently, I found a job in another city where jobs are few. Although it required me to commute one hundred and twenty miles round trip every day, I felt fortunate to be working.

The company I worked for was a fledgling company filled with young people my age who loved to party. There were beer parties on premises after work, drinking over lunch hours, and more frequently than not, a ready supply of cocaine. Once again, I found myself living a shame-based life trapped by the helplessness of my own patterns and choices. Daily I found myself guzzling a six-pack of beer – my only passenger on the sixty-mile stretch of highway to my home. By the time I arrived at my little town, I had lost all capacity to make any choice other than to continue past my trailer house to the corner bar where I would spend the remainder of my evening.

This was my life for one hundred and twenty miles round trip *every* workday for six months: driving to work hung over, driving home drunk, and passing my trailer home and going straight to the bar until closing time. Just to get up the next day and repeat the dance.

"Dear God, help me! Tonight I promise to go straight home, make myself a hearty meal, pay a few bills, and get a good night's sleep."

During one pivotal one-hundred-and-twenty-mile commute – six months and about 150 prayers later – something happened. My prayer was answered. God didn't magically pluck me out of my insanity, but God did appear to me in the form of a new insight I had never considered before.

What I say to you next might sound strange, but first a preamble...

For months, perhaps because I was on the suicidal track of driving drunk, my mind was preoccupied with thoughts about death. The question that kept coming to me was, "What happens when we die?"

I was compelled to learn more about death and dying. I became absorbed in stories of people who had re-entered life after having been considered clinically dead. The most common experience reported was that of being enveloped and guided by a brilliant white light that bathed them in an indescribable feeling of love. Upon returning to consciousness, many of these people emerged with an awakened and more vibrant relationship to God and to life. Within them was instilled a certainty that the purpose of life is to express love through fearless engagement with life and service to others.

I was awed by the power of this Light to both direct people back from the edge of death and leave in its footprint an even greater gift — purposeful direction with love as its foundation.

In the final few miles of one fateful one-hundred-and-twenty-mile daily trek, my "inner sight" cleared momentarily as I awoke to the realization that I had made my addictions more powerful than the Light. In that epiphany, something within me spoke:

"Any attachment to illusion will prevent you from seeing and following the Light. The more strongly you are attached to anything in the physical realm, the greater the likelihood that you will mistake that attachment for what is real."

Attachment is like a bright shiny trinket covering a black hole of despair. The illusion is that joy and peace can be found at its center.

In a moment of clarity I knew that I had been seeking something real in a place of smoke and mirrors whose only promise was pain. With great certainty, I knew that I would be lost, both in life and in death, if I did not choose "The Real." Along with that certainty, came a wisdom and a strength that set me on a path to an ever-evolving spiritual transformation that allows me to celebrate today — twenty-six years later — a recovered life.

Looking back, what I know for sure is that all the people, challenges, failures, and frustrations conspired to bring me to my knees so that I could discover the true Source of a life of magnificence, awe, wonder, and contribution. Today, sustaining a recovered life calls for me to intentionally nurture a conscious partnership with the Divine as

God, and as it manifests itself in and through my human relationships and my daily circumstances.

Through God's partnership and grace, I have gained wisdom, experience, compassion, and love. These gifts and more, I express in joyful and grateful service to others. Borrowing from Gandhi, I find myself living his truth: "My life is my message." Indeed, my life AS my message is all that I have to give.

My "one hundred and twenty miles" was the road from addiction to spiritual transformation. For each of you, it is life by default.

It is the hypnotic trance under which you live – disconnected from self, disconnected from Spirit. You can recognize this road in several ways:

1. By examining the places within you that cause you to suffer and leave you feeling unfulfilled, desperate, and impotent

2. By questioning the meaning of your existence and your place in it

3. By acknowledging the patterns in your thoughts and behaviors that keep you trapped in a vicious cycle of hopelessness

4. By surfacing the nature of your attachments. You may not be attached, as I was, to physical substances, but you may find that you are attached to people, self-limiting habits, and even your opinions about the way things are, the way you are, or the way others are. These attachments are based in fear and will cause you not to see "The Real." They will bring you no satisfaction or joy and will keep you lost.

These areas of tension within you are your wake-up call. Paradoxically, "one hundred and twenty miles" is also your way out. It is the road not taken. Its path is steep, covered over with weeds, and strewn with rocks. It is the warrior's way. For once you set foot on this path with God, awake and alive with intention, you will be called to give up who you are for who you can become. And that is a moment-to-moment choice that is worthy of fighting for.

At the end of this road is the true destination you seek.

Sandye Brown, Master Certified Coach, is the founder of Wide Awake, Inc., a transformational personal and leadership development firm based in Vancouver, Washington. Sandye is known nationally for her work as a personal transformation architect and executive coach whose mission is helping people actualize their purpose through the process of their own transformation. Working from a holistic perspective, Sandye's unique approach changes people from the inside out. For more information on Sandye, please visit www.WideAwakeInc.com.

From an Addict to an Intuitive Life Coach

Shamala Tan

"GET UP! OR ELSE I WILL KICK YOUR FACE IN!" I shouted down at him gleefully.

As I looked down at him, I saw the elevator door slamming against his head continuously, not hard, but hard enough to move his head back and forth. He was lying on the floor with his head sticking out of the elevator. He had passed out. K and I giggled. We could not help it even though we knew it was unkind to do so. We just could not control ourselves.

"Shh... let's not attract attention," said K.

"Should we call someone?" I asked, trying to see the seriousness of the situation.

"That will get us into trouble!" retorted K.

"So what should we do with him?" I asked, as I poked G's back with my foot. Then both of us burst into giggles again.

"Let's drag him back into the elevator, then up to your apartment, and see if he wakes up," I suggested.

Four hours later I felt myself stirring. I was waking up, but wait… I was not on my bed.

"What am I doing sitting here?" I thought. I looked around me and saw that I was at a wine bar with people I did not know. I could not make out what they were saying. I felt deaf — as if the whole world around me was muted. The people at my table looked at me and then continued with their conversation. I felt alone. Scared. I recognized that I was at my regular haunt, and then I remembered I had come here with K and a bunch of other people. I looked at my watch. It was 3:00 am.

I don't know how long I sat there, but I was feeling very uncomfortable, as I didn't know these people I was sitting with. Was I having a conversation with them before I "woke up?" How did this happen? I spotted K at a distance. I waved, but she didn't see me.

I looked at my watch nervously again. It was now 3:30 am. A voice inside me said, "Go home. Leave now."

I stood up and ran to the taxi stand.

That was a day in my life from what feels like a lifetime ago. My life then was filled with drunken blackouts, feeling lost, and not knowing how I got home or who I went out with. The constant sense of disorientation, heavy heart, guilt, self-loathing, and a deep sense of inner sickness filled me and my aura. I could deal with a real physical sickness, but the inner sickness was beyond me.

I often woke up in the morning with a deep sense of regret, and vowed not to do it again. But when night came I was back drinking my poison. They say that one of the signs of an alcoholic is the desire to drink alone. For me drinking was no longer a social activity, it was a necessity, and I drank alone at home often.

This was my story. Well, it was only half of my true story. Let me explain.

When I first submitted my chapter for this book, I thought it was enough. However, my story was incomplete, as I did not share everything. So when the editor asked me to re-write on the first edit, I knew that I had to be transparent and share my whole story.

What I am about to share with you is not something I have kept from other people; it is by no means a secret. In fact this story is twenty years old. I have shared it with many people, especially if I felt that my story could help them, but I stopped talking about it a long time ago as my story was judged, misunderstood, and it made other people uncomfortable.

So here I am again sharing this story, hoping to reach out to the right people who will find strength from my story in their own transformational process.

As you may have guessed, my alcohol dependence did not just happen on its own. In my late teens and early twenties, I took to the clubbing circuit and enjoyed the crazy life it offered.

Through the party circuit I met someone I liked, and after two dates I really wanted to see more of him. He took advantage of this and our relationship then took a strange turn. He began to treat me with warm affection one day, and then coldness the next. It was something different every time I saw him. Sometimes he would call me at my office countless times like a caring boyfriend; other times he would not return my calls for days. Some days he would praise me and other days criticize me. I would feel deflated when criticized and say to myself, "This relationship is not right for me," and as if he had read my mind, he would immediately change his tune and start being loving to me again. So it gave me hope that the relationship would work, but it was the most confusing relationship I had had, if you could even call it a relationship.

In all of this emotional and mental turmoil, he also raped me. Twice.

By this time my self-confidence, self-esteem, and self-body image plummeted. I felt violated emotionally and mentally more than physically. When he disappeared from my life, I was relieved, even though I was lost. I had no direction in life.

I kept asking myself, "How could I have been so stupid? I should have seen it coming." I saw a counselor eight months after we broke up, but I kept the self who was being counseled separate from the one who lived the party circuit.

I took to drinking because it was available. As a drunk I was abusive to taxi drivers, other pub-crawlers, and strangers. Basically I became a nuisance to society. My dependence on alcohol lasted for close to ten years.

I remember the day I decided to stop drinking for good after not knowing how I got home the night before – again, for the umpteenth time. I felt an inner strength stirring, and today I still do not intellectually know where it came from.

At that time I began to have the most bizarre dreams. The strength stirring within was somehow connected to the dreams I was about to experience for the next few months of my new life.

The dreams were uplifting, healing, and very much part of a deep spiritual awakening. I experienced tremendous healing when I dreamt of a well-known Indian spiritual guru visiting in my home. In my semi-sleep state I also saw celestial beings convening in my living room, attempting to communicate with me.

I was bewildered by the dream experiences. Did I dream them or imagine them? Was this the aftereffect of giving up alcohol? All I knew was that my life changed forever after the series of dreams.

For a period of several months, my dream world and my waking world merged intermittently. I looked forward to going to bed, as the dreams revealed to me unlimited possibilities and how they could positively affect my waking reality.

I could go on to describe the dream experiences, but I know that my words would fail me. It was one of those things that you just had to experience to appreciate. And of course, they were my dreams, and no one else could ever experience them the way I did. How can I possibly describe faithfully the beautiful sounds of heaven being played in my ears as I awoke one morning, without sounding like I have gone crazy?

Good things were happening to me, and that was enough for me. Day by day the world looked different to me. My deep self-loathing slowly evaporated. I worked on loving myself and accepting my body image, and most important, I forgave myself. Making the decision to love and forgive myself was a very difficult thing to do. Not because I didn't want to, but because I hadn't realized that I was not loving myself, and I didn't know that I was punishing myself through my self-destructive actions.

During my recovery, I spent hours in meditation, read many spiritual transformational books, and applied what I learned to my life in order to change myself. I learned that one can never learn and acquire wisdom if one does not apply the information. I grasped at whatever I could to get better. Through my journey, I saw the value in all the difficult lessons of being in abusive relationships, dealing with addictions, becoming a nuisance to society, and, most of all, dealing with my biggest enemy – myself.

Today I am happily married to a wonderful and very spiritual man, and we have a beautiful daughter. Looking back, I feel as if the one who was lost and burdened was someone I knew a lifetime ago.

I believe that everyone is given second, third, or fourth chances in life. We all make mistakes, and sometimes very destructive ones, but if we are willing to face ourselves and deal with the most difficult parts of ourselves, we will open up to deep inner transformational healing that is divinely orchestrated and inspired.

I feel blessed to be in a position now to help others with their metamorphoses. The gift from the Universe to me is to set butterflies free...

Shamala Tan is an intuitive life coach with expertise in helping others to realize their purpose. Throughout her twenties, Shamala was an alcoholic, but her recovery led her to a journey of inner transformation that inspired her to coach others on purpose realization. Today she also coaches solo entrepreneurs on how to run profitable businesses with love. Visit www.BeSpiritualAndRich.com to download an abundance meditation and information about how to fulfill your purpose.

In the Heart of You Is God

Simran Sofia Love

The Scream of Consciousness

AS I STOOD ALONE IN THE MIDDLE of the living room of my deceased grandmother's house, I screamed so loudly that I lost my voice. Even in my state of desperation, I noticed internal surprise at the loudness and intensity of the scream. It was followed by an even louder silence, as if time ceased to exist in that very instant. For a moment I thought I had gone deaf.

At age twenty-six, I found myself bedridden, sleeping for twenty hours a day, and unable to walk for weeks at a time due to extreme pain and exhaustion. I had come to live alone in my late grandmother's empty house a few months previously to die, but my soul resisted. I was desperate to get out of my own skin. As my depression, frustration, anger, and fear built up to an unbearable level, I screamed at God for a way out.

A year earlier, two months into my senior year in college, increasing health problems had lead to a collapse of my immune

255

system. I loved my studies in fine art, and had dreamed of attending this particular art college since I had been twelve years old. Even before college, I had no problems getting my artwork into exhibitions in which most of my paintings and prints sold. It simply did not make any sense that my body was giving up on me just as my life was beginning.

At that point I made a deal with God, that if I could only live long enough to finish college, I would not mind at all to die afterwards. During my senior year, unable to walk into college, I spent most of my time in bed making small sculptures for my final exhibition, shifting between feelings of ecstasy at being alive, and deep depression and despair.

So there I was, with a beautiful degree from a high-prestige art college, but struck with dis-ease to such an extent that I could not work to provide for myself, nor was there any medical doctor who could help me. My symptoms did not resonate with anything that is taught in medical school, so I had long since stopped seeking help from anyone in the standard medical profession. All I got from presenting symptoms not understood or recognized was humiliation. I could not stand it.

My higher self had been nudging me to look into alternative medicine while I was in college, and based on my research, I had changed my diet and started taking a whole range of natural supplements. While this was certainly much more productive in terms of pain relief, my health kept deteriorating. My body was dying, but my soul refused to let go. I could not understand why, or find any meaning to my suffering – it was just meaningless and I was stuck in it. So at a loss for a better alternative, I screamed my frustration at God. Little did I know at the time that my scream was heard.

An Angel in Disguise

Shortly after my outburst at God, my brother phoned me about someone he thought might be able to help me. With financial aid from my family, I was able to travel from my grandmother's nest in the countryside to the big city, and a meeting that changed everything. An angel in disguise entered my life.

After checking my blood in a dark-field microscope, the man I had come to see looked rather concerned. Not surprisingly, there was no life force energy in my blood. The tests revealed that I had a lung dis-ease that had spread to all vital organs. No wonder I was in so much pain. No wonder I couldn't digest any food.

I was prescribed several natural remedies that I immediately started taking. I did not know this at the time, but this man did not think I was going to live. Only four years later when he very happily exclaimed that he was no longer concerned that I would die, did I understand why every week, and sometimes daily since we had first met, he had phoned me. He was checking to see if I was still alive. The memory of his empathy and kindness moves me to this day. An angel, for sure, heard my scream.

The Magic of Consciousness

There is a saying that the Universe never serves you any challenge greater than what you can handle. I have certainly wondered about that one during the more stressful times in my life. Trust and receptivity are two necessities needed to handle challenges, and I discovered this deep down at the core of my being during my healing journey.

Once I allowed myself to trust life sufficiently to be receptive, I was provided with amazing support.

When I finally discovered what was going on with my body physically, I transformed my whole direction and outlook on life. The very moment I took conscious charge and responsibility of my healing process, I realized how I had created dis-ease, which means to disallow ease, in my body with my thoughts and emotions. I used to believe the outside world controlled me, that life was something that happened to me. It was a grim, fear-based reality of dis-ease, abuse, and depression, and feelings of separation and lack of control. I felt like a victim — a victim of life, a victim of my genes, and a victim of circumstances. By the time I was fifteen years old, I was so incredibly disempowered by my belief systems that I wanted to die. Within a decade, my body collapsed, mirroring my distorted mind.

As the empowered realization that I create my life slowly dawned upon me, I finally understood what was going on. My body was screaming me into awareness with all its pain and symptoms. Never had I felt such gratitude for my body than in this moment of realization. My body was simply trying to communicate with me. What a relief! I had never been a victim of circumstances, and my body was not weak. I could, in fact, choose my own directions and reactions in life, and I could heal my body through the magic of my ever-evolving consciousness.

In the Heart of You Is God

It took me a few years, but in my second decade after screaming my frustration at God, I now live my life in the full knowing that anything is possible. I am living proof that you can heal your body from serious dis-ease and really transform your way of being in the world.

I fully believe that I create my reality based on my level of consciousness. In fact, I co-create my reality with the same creative power that has created me. As you, I am an infinite being, and limitless creation is my birthright.

How did I come to this knowing, this inner realization that anything is possible, and have the strength to change my mindset while being so ill? After being introduced to my lifeless blood in the dark-field microscope all those years ago, I gathered all the information I could find about how to increase my life force energy and vitality, not only physically, but on all levels, as this seemed to be my missing link to a healthy and vibrant life. I started recognizing that everything is energy vibrating on different frequencies, and simply a reflection of consciousness. I knew that if this were true, my body would have to heal once I increased my flow of high-vibration life force energy.

After making some very conscious changes in what I fed my mind and body, which involved eating raw vegan food and flooding myself with positive thinking, my body healed and my perspective and outlook on life shifted. High-vibration, living food became an amazing tool to transform everything in my life. It makes perfect sense to me that if you feed your mind and body with low-vibration energy, meaning lifeless, negative, toxic energy, in time they wither and die. Your food, thoughts, and emotions are the most significant energy you feed your body and your life with, and to thrive, life needs high-vibration energy.

Many years and transformations later, I know that the high-vibration energy that created me and every living being around me, be it a person, an animal, or a leaf on a tree, is an omnipresent life force energy that sustains, heals, and nourishes all life. I can choose to let it in completely, or reduce the flow. It is always an unconditional, abundant, and obedient energy. This energy resides in your essence — your soul, your heart-space — and creates reminders that you, as a part of God, are free to express and create anything you wish. Just think for a moment what an amazing series of synchronicities it has taken for you to hold this book in your hands right now so that you could be inspired by these stories. Surely it is the creation of a master.

Bless you. We are all one.

Simran Sofia Love is a mother, artist, transformational author, entrepreneur, visionary, life coach, raw nutrition expert, holistic teacher, and natural therapist specializing in energy medicine. She is the author of *Raw Body Cleanse: Cleanse Your Body — Transform Your Life*. Her next books, titled *In the Heart of You Is God* and *Emilie's World: Raw Food for Children,* are due in 2013. For free gifts, newsletters, and product information, please visit www.TheHolisticRawFoodCoach.com and www.RawHolisticMom.com.

The Choice That Changed Everything

Sonia Choquette

I BELIEVE THAT EVERYONE EXPERIENCES a pivotal moment in their life when something totally unexpected happens which causes each of us to stop, really examine where we're going on this journey, and make course corrections to start living a purpose-driven existence. Call it a transformation or an awakening – whatever you'd like to name it. If you've not had such an experience, believe me, it will come your way at some point in time, just as it did in my own life.

I was on a cross country tour promoting my third book titled *The Wise Child* (which has since been renamed *The Intuitive Spark: Nurturing Intuition in Your Child, Your Family and You*) when I experienced my own wake-up call.

I should mention that these were the days before Facebook, social media, and all the modern tools of marketing were in existence. Basically I travelled from city to city, hopeful and optimistic about saving the world and saving the children through my book, only to be met with small crowds at book signings. This was a huge blow to my ego and it was a tough time in my life. Not only that, I was travelling with a gentleman I had met at a workshop who was a musician, so of course, he also had delusions of grandeur about travelling and meeting masses of people, which unfortunately wasn't happening.

The lowest point came in San Francisco one rainy evening. We arrived at a bookstore on Union Street where there were forty chairs lined up for people to hear me speak about my book... and there was only one homeless man seated in the first row. Mark said, "Well, let's go." And I said, "No, we can't go." He replied, "What do you mean we can't go?" I said, "Look, it's not about what's out there. I have to do what I do and you have to do what you do, and the Universe will take care of the rest." "So what you mean is we're going to talk to the homeless man?" And I said, "Yes. That's what we're here to do."

I proceeded to talk to him as if I were talking to a thousand people, and then had my musician friend sing to him. At one point, he looked up at me and winked. The rest of the time he was literally snoring in his chair. I laughed at that wink and looked to Mark and said, "Maybe he's an angel." But then, even he got up and left. And all that was left behind was a wisp of urine and stinkiness.

We went across the street and I cried. Mark comforted me and then he cried. I comforted him and I said, "Well, you know what Mark? All we can ever do in life is do what we do with love. And that's it." That was the beginning of my personal transformation.

Let's fast forward. Years passed, and unbeknownst to me, the woman who was the manager of that bookstore had left that position and gone to a store called East West Bookstore in Mountain View. A gentleman came in one day and said to her, "Look, I just got a new job recruiting new talent. Who would you recommend in the spiritual book field?" And she said, "Well, the only person I would recommend is Sonia Choquette. A while back she came to speak at another bookstore where I used to work, but no one showed up. Instead of being angry and upset and blaming me, she gave the best talk of her life to a homeless man as though the room was full. And that was so impressive."

That man went back to his publisher, which happened to be Hay House. They recruited me, and said, "We heard about you from this one event, and we would like to invite you to join our house. We will send you on tours around the world and support you in every way we can because you're the kind of person that we believe in and what Hay House is about." My career exploded.

That night when no one showed up to hear me speak was truly that moment when I could have left my career behind, injured, pissed, hurt, rejected, mad, any of the above, but instead I decided to do what I do because that's all I can do. And I think that homeless man was an angel. My life has been transformed. I'm now published in thirty-five countries. I am travelling all over the world doing what I love for very gorgeous international audiences. And I have to say, had I given up that day, had I not offered my message with the love that was in my book to that sole occupant in the room, I would not be where I am today.

One of my primary messages that I try to impart to my readers is that living your spirit in integrity and being of service to the planet is inherent to your well-being. We are all messengers here to deliver wisdom. It's not about asking the Universe, "Hey, what can YOU give me?" but rather about serving others. Don't worry about who's in the audience. If I'd have let that experience of the disastrous book signing dictate the course of my life, I would have betrayed everything that I have ever written about and become an instant fraud. As hard as it was, it never occurred to me to leave. I was there to give a message.

I was blessed to have had an amazing teacher years ago whom I've written about in my book *The Diary of a Psychic*. Charlie Goodman was my first mentor when I started being mentored to do intuitive work. Once he said to me, "Sonia, your job is to mind your own business. Just do your business and don't worry about what's out there." So if your business is to be the teacher, the writer, or the messenger, give the message and don't worry about how it's received. Just give it the best you can with love.

I was twelve when I heard that message, but it went straight into my heart and it is definitely how I have lived my whole life ever since. And I will say it has been a good message to live by. I had to wait several years before I experienced my redemptive moment, and I was still surprised when the moment of enlightenment came about. You never know when this special moment will happen, and especially as an author, don't judge your value or your success by who's there in front of you in the moment. You don't know what's really happening in the big picture. Give your message with love, do your best, and be more interested in giving than in what you are going to receive from sharing your presence with the world.

I'd like to share with you another transformational moment in my life that led up to my eventual work in my life, which also involved the wonderful Charlie Goodman. He'd told me that he would mentor me and I was to meet him at 7:00 pm on Fridays, and I agreed.

For two weeks I arrived exactly at 7:00 pm at his place, but the third week I was a little late getting there. When I rang the doorbell, no one came to the door. At first I thought he'd just forgotten our meeting, so I rang the doorbell again. Then I thought, "Well, maybe he fell asleep," so I rang it again. Next I thought, "Maybe he's dead," and kept ringing the bell. Still no answer. I just left, thinking, "He let me down."

The following week arrived and I didn't know what to do. I decided to arrive early at his house, and sat on his porch until 7:00 pm, at which time I rang his doorbell. He opened the door and I said, "Oh my God, you're alive! Where were you? I thought you were dead!" And he asked, "Why would you think that?" I responded, "Well, I came here last week and you weren't here. Did you forget?" He replied, "No, I didn't forget. We had an appointment at 7:00 pm. You were not here at 7:00 pm, so I left at 7:10 pm."

It had never occurred to me that I was the problem. And so I learned about value. He taught me the value of my word, the value of integrity, and the values of being responsible, doing what I do, committing my time, and committing other people's time.

And so when I went to that bookstore, the manager had invested in me. I didn't care if nobody showed up. I would have sat there until eight o'clock. Never would it have occurred to me to look at her as if she had failed.

I think that the appointment with Charlie was another defining moment. It never occurred to me at that age that his not being there was my failure. Charlie brought it so lovingly to my attention, and laughed, saying, "Let's go. Let's get started."

And that, for me, was another moment – a lesson, if you will. It taught me that before I jump so quickly to transfer ownership of a situation to another by saying, "You didn't do what you were supposed to do for me," I need to slow down and take possession of my actions. That bookstore owner who had recommended me said that my lack of blaming was such a shock to her. She was prepared for me to come after her, because so many authors would have, for not ensuring that people were there to hear me speak. My reaction was, "Really? Wow. That's a compliment."

I realized then that to be a writer, to be in the world to share your message, is such a privilege. I am so grateful that I do know that it's a work of service.

I've had many "aha!" moments, but I'll share one more with you. In my early twenties, right out of college, I was so interested in travelling that I joined an airline and became a flight attendant. It was miserable work and was not for me. I stuck it out, but I took a lot of leaves of absence. And then the airline I worked for went on strike, and I didn't have a job to go to. I could go picket with the other employees, but it was a drag to do so for a job that I didn't love.

Eventually the strike ended and we didn't get our jobs back. But I got a job offer from another airline. Out of the blue they sent me a letter that basically said, "We'll give you the job." I was about a mile away from where the interview was to be held when I turned around and went home. My first thought was, "I hate this job. It's not for me." And next I thought, "It would be selfish of me to take that job that could belong to someone else who would be perfect for it and who would love doing this work." So I just went home, cancelled, and had no job. I told myself, "Okay. I'm going to just keep doing what I do. I'm going to do intuitive work and offer some classes. And I'm just going to tough it out."

Within that month, a fellow came to one of my classes — a

class that actually turned out to be my first book, *The Psychic Pathway*. He was a freelance writer and was so taken with my work that he wrote an article about me. It went on the cover of a Chicago magazine called *The Reader*, and it was one of the longest articles they had ever published.

I was an instant local celebrity, and the article got picked up by the *Chicago Tribune*. So now I was even more of a local celebrity. Then it got picked up by nationally syndicated news services. Within thirty days I was a national celebrity, and received over 3,500 phone calls from people who wanted to know more about my work or study with me. All this happened in thirty days. And I have never looked back.

I need to be perfectly honest here and tell you that during the airline attendant fiasco, I was giving up in my mind when I turned around on the way to that interview and went home. Imagine free passes to travel the world from an even bigger airline, health insurance, and part-time work – because essentially I only had to work, by contract, seventeen to eighteen days a month, albeit there would have been days away from home. It was a lot for me to consider, but the truth was it wasn't me. And my husband was not happy. He asked, "What do you mean you didn't go to the interview?" But he accepted my decision. The part he was looking at, the health insurance, free travel, a lot of benefits, was so attractive to him, but he said, "Okay." That was that, and we never talked about it again.

Within a month, I'd moved on to a new thing, and that's the path I've been on ever since. My life's plan has been comprised of nothing but those defining moments.

One of my sincerest hopes is that people will recognize that we create our own world experience, both personally and for our collective world. Each one of us should create our path from a place of our heart, love, integrity, authenticity, and willingness to serve, instead of being led by our fear, greed, smallness, and selfishness. If we strive to serve the world this way, then we will all be okay. And it starts one person at a time.

I stayed at that bookstore, and I now know that I've affected at least a million people from that one decision, based on how many books I've sold since I made that choice. It's mind-boggling to me.

I'd like to leave you with one small piece of wisdom: Stay true to your heart, because there's always a bigger picture than what is revealed in the moment.

Your true path awaits you.

Sonia Choquette is a world-renowned author, storyteller, vibrational healer, and six sensory spiritual teacher, in international demand for her guidance, wisdom, and capacity to heal the soul. Her books have sold over a million copies worldwide including her *New York Times* bestseller, *The Answer Is Simple...Love Yourself, Live Your Spirit*. She is most recognized for her ability to instantly change vibration, lift depression, and connect others to their intuition. She helps people understand their soul's plan and purpose, and leads them to successful, meaningful, and peaceful lives. For more information, visit www.SoniaChoquette.com.

BECOME A FEATURED AUTHOR IN
THE NEXT VOLUME OF

Pebbles in the Pond
Transforming the World One Person at a Time

If you want to share your story in the next volume in this series, and believe in the powerful impact one voice (*your story*) can have to truly make a difference, then I want to hear from you!

Ask any one of the authors in this book and they'll tell you that it's been a life-changing experience to be a contributing author to *Pebbles in the Pond*. Beyond the accomplishment of getting published alongside some of today's most successful authors, you'll become part of a powerful Mastermind "family," or as we've come to call it – a MasterHeart.

You'll make valuable connections and life-long friendships with like-minded authors, as well as receive eight months of guidance and coaching to help you write your chapter, get started as a Transformational Author, and learn how to market a book from the ground up.

You'll work with a professional editor to polish your chapter (so don't fret if you feel your writing isn't "perfect" – nobody's is). And you'll receive an additional six months of coaching in my award-winning *Get Your Book*

Done® program to write your own book. Plus, you'll receive free attendance at the famous *Transformational Author Retreat* (a three-day retreat with your fellow contributors that includes all meals and accommodations). Of course, you'll also receive your own copies of the next *Pebbles in the Pond* book – the one you will be in – to sell!

If you are interested in applying to be a contributor to the next volume, please email info@transformationalauthor.com right away to request an application.

I hope to have the opportunity to work with you, and to see your story in the next book!

Many blessings,

Christine Kloser

Spiritual Guide ~ Award-Winning Author
Transformational Book Coach
President, Transformation Books

Connect with the Authors

Website: www.PebblesInThePondBook.com

Blog: www.PebblesInThePondBook.com/category/blog/

Facebook: www.Facebook.com/pebblesinthepond

You Tube: www.YouTube.com/pebblesinthepondbook

Cinch: www.cinch.fm/pebbles-in-the-pond-book

About Christine Kloser

Christine Kloser is a spiritual guide, award-winning author, and Transformational Book Coach whose spot-on guidance transforms the lives of visionary entrepreneurs and authors around the world. Her passion is fueled by her own transformation in December of 2010, when after much success as an entrepreneur, she found herself curled up in a ball on the floor sobbing because she had lost it all. Letting go of the last shred of stability and security in her life, she discovered her Truth and the blessings began to flow.

From that place, she courageously (and faithfully) went on to create the most abundant, impactful, and joyous success of her life in a matter of a few short months. Christine knows how to flip the switch from stressed to blessed, and loves sharing her wisdom in everything she does, from writing and speaking to coaching and training

In addition to her work with clients from every corner of the world, Christine has been featured in the *Los Angeles Times, Entrepreneur Magazine, Atlanta Constitution-Journal, Leadership Excellence, FOX News*, Forbes.com, and Entrepreneur.com, and is a regular columnist for *PUBLISHED! Magazine*. Her books and publications have received numerous awards including the Nautilus Book Silver Award, Pinnacle Book Award, National Best Books Award, and the Apex Award for Publication Excellence.

After living in Los Angeles, California for fourteen years, Christine now resides in York, Pennsylvania with her husband David, and daughter, Janet, where they enjoy a much slower-paced and relaxed lifestyle.